FIERCE *Integrity*

A COURSE IN LIVING YOUR TRUTH

MAREN  HASSE

The **Difference** PRESS

DEDICATION

For Brent

whose memory will forever remind
me to stand in the light.

To have the courage to be more of me
than I was the day before.

To live with
FIERCE Integrity

Shakakan brother.

ADVANCE PRAISE

"There are moments in our lives where we discover a light in our unconscious selves, and suddenly we examine, exclaim, and remark over what we discover. Shining it into the depths of our beings, we awaken to who we are, have gratitude for where we have been, and faith in the path that lies before us. Realizing the mystery of divinity, possibility and power has been at our fingertips all along! They have been called 'Aha' moments... and are known to be the food that feeds the soul. Maren Hasse and the Fierce Integrity Project are one such light.

This project and its teachings illuminate the secret behind all of your suffering.... You. Knowing that at a core level you already have all you are seeking, it is merely a matter of sifting through what has gotten in your way. Within these chapters lies an opportunity to align your life with the truth of your soul. Through courage, determination, and humbleness you will be transformed.

Sharing her own personal story offers a powerful reflection, as we see that each of us goes through the 'not good enough, perfectionism, unworthiness' issues in our own ways, and it is up to us to shed the victim stories to manifest change.

Maren is thorough in her recognition of your need to come into balance with all you are in relationship with; from the food you eat, the events that have formed you, the people you surround yourself with, and the work that you do. She guides you with questions and actions to begin a conversation that matters. Teaching the power of present minded observation and heart focus, so the thoughts which cloud your vision and choices become still... The words that you speak become conscious... the way that you live authentic... until you are living and breathing Integrity.

This is the Fierce Integrity Project"

Sarah Salter Kelly
Shaman, Writer, Mystic

"FIERCE Integrity is one of the clearest and most thoughtful books I've ever read. Author Maren Hasse will take you on an intensely personal journey of discovery but she doesn't stop there. She has broken down her experience into a message that will give you deep personal insights and change the way you look at your life, your relationships, and your own path. This is a book that you will be reading again and again."

Aaron Paquette
First Nations Metis Artist, Writer, Presenter

TABLE OF CONTENTS

PREFACE

Sitting with my eyes closed, I feel my body begin to relax as I am carried away by the words of the guided meditation. My face and belly soften and my breathing takes on a slow, deep, and calm rhythm. As my body begins to rest, my mind's eye begins to awaken as beautiful, colorful images start to flood my inner vision, becoming my temporary reality. I am no longer contained by the vessel that is my body as I feel my consciousness continue to expand, following the words of the Shaman deeper and deeper into the journey. It is a shapeshifting journey, one in which I am morphing from form to form, animal to animal, entity to entity. Beginning in the ocean where I am a dolphin, I can practically feel the water on my smooth skin and the joy bubbling in my heart. I become a salmon jumping upstream, feeling the strength and stamina that are necessary to complete this arduous task, but also the urgency of my calling upriver. I become a bear, nourishing my strong body with the flesh of the salmon and I feel overwhelmed with gratitude. The shapeshifting continues until I find myself in a cave, deep, deep within Mother Earth. There is a fire lit there and I follow the light closer and closer until I am surrounded by other beings, the Ancestors, and I begin to move around the fire with them, drumming, dancing, and chanting.

One of the Ancestors calls to me, asking me to join him seated next to the fire. I cannot discern his face but I can feel his energy;

it is peaceful, loving, safe. I take my place next to him as the others continue to dance and move around us, enfolding us in this sacred space.

"What is it that you wish to ask me?" I hear his question in my mind although his lips do not move.

I don't answer. My mind bubbles to life as it starts to run through the possibilities...the project, being of Service, my deep desire to help others. I am distracted momentarily by the increasing tempo of the drumming and dancing. Before I can decide how to frame the question that I want to ask, the Being speaks again.

"Integrity. Fierce Integrity." And with that, the fire begins to dim and the music begins to fade. The Ancestors are gone, and before I have a chance to even process what is happening, I am sitting back on the beach where my journey began.

Opening up my eyes, I look out into the faces of those around me. Bradley, the Shaman who led us on the journey, begins to lead a discussion. I am trying to stay present for the discussion but my mind is reeling.

"Integrity? Fierce Integrity? What does that MEAN?!" (My ego is alive and well and in fine form).

I am hesitant to share too much about my journey, but I do feel compelled to express the vividness of my experience, the shapeshifting. Never before has a journey been so real, so clear, so full of feeling. I am almost moved to tears as I try to describe the experience, and feeling slightly embarrassed, I quickly end my turn before I say too much.

I struggle to listen to the rest of the participants and I am relieved when we wrap up for the evening and I can retreat to the solitude of my car. I put the key into the ignition but I don't start it. I find myself sitting still. Breathing. Listening. Thinking.

I am not sure how long I sit like this, but eventually I shake myself back to the present and start the car. I start driving home, still thinking.

"There was something so familiar about that Being, but I can't seem to put my finger on it."

I am frustrated that I couldn't see his face. Come to think of it, I couldn't see anyone's face in the cave. And yet, I felt safe, comfortable, loved.

The realization hits me so hard that I almost drive off the road.

"Brent. Oh my God, Brent."

The magnitude of this realization shakes me to my core and my mind kicks into overdrive.

"What did he mean by Fierce Integrity? Why couldn't I see his face? Why didn't I know it was him? Why couldn't I have stayed longer? I have so much to say!"

I pull into my driveway, my mind filled with unanswered questions. I idly check my phone for messages and the date and time appear on the screen. I am frozen. Incredulous. It is May 2, 2012. Exactly one year since the date of Brent's passing.

TO EXPERIENCE YOUR OWN VERSION OF A SHAMANIC-STYLE JOURNEY, GUIDED BY MAREN HASSE VISIT, WWW.FIERCEINTEGRITYBOOK.COM

ACKNOWLEDGEMENTS

Writing this book has been a wondrous journey, a healing journey. I am very grateful for having had the opportunity and space to simply step into the flow and allow it to happen. It has been first and foremost an act of Divine Grace.

TO TRENT — Thank you for your love, support, and patience over our years together. What a ride it has been. You are an amazing man and I am one lucky lady to be sharing in this life with you.

TO CHEPHREN — What a gift you are in my life! From the moment you were conceived, my heart was full. It was, and is, eternally yours. I love being your mama more than anything.

TO MY MOM & DAD — The gratitude I feel towards each of you is beyond words. You define what it means to live with FIERCE Integrity. Thank you for holding the light and showing me the way. I love you both so very, very much.

TO ERIK & BEN — I am humbled and honored to be on this journey with you. Being your sister is a great privilege and honor.

TO MY DAD ROSS — We are forever connected as father and daughter, and I wouldn't change a thing.

To my Nordegg family — What an amazing community of people you are! I relish the time I get to spend with each and every one of you. There must be something in the water...

To my friend Krista — Thank you so very much for your support and your editing efforts. Your generosity of time and spirit have meant so very much to me.

To Jo Anna — I want to laugh and laugh when I think of all of the synchronicities that brought us together. What a gem you are as a coach! Thanks for holding the space for me to turn the "five year plan" into "six months of magic." Looking forward to the next six.

To my first readers club — Thank you so much for your time, energy, and contributions. I value all of your opinions dearly.

To Lynn — I am so very glad that the Universe put us together to work on this project! You are a light in this world and I am so very grateful that I have had the privilege to work with you.

To Angela, Ann, Jessie and all of the people at Difference Press — Thank you for believing in this work and for guiding me through the publishing process. If it wasn't for you, I would still be sitting here dumbfounded, holding onto this manuscript and wondering what on earth I was supposed to do with it!

Finally,

To Brent. You are never very far, my friend. I am eternally grateful for having had the opportunity to know you. Your memory will continue to inspire me for the rest of my days.

INTRODUCTION:

How to use this book

This is a book, a course actually, on living with Integrity. The first thing to ask yourself then, is "What is Integrity?" For a lot of people, having Integrity means to tell the truth—and while this is certainly part of living with Integrity, it is only one part of the equation. As you will see in this course, Integrity involves more than just our words. It also involves our thoughts and our actions. For me, living with Integrity means being honest in thought, word, and deed. It means telling yourself the truth first (your thoughts), telling that same truth to others (your word), and then matching your behavior with both your thoughts and your words (your actions or deed).

There is another definition of Integrity that comes into play as well, and that is the idea that to have Integrity means to be whole. In this meaning of Integrity, when someone or something has Integrity, they are undamaged, undiminished, or not less than. I like this definition, because I believe that when you begin to live with Integrity of thought, word, and deed—what I call FIERCE Integrity—you become more whole. You become more "you" than you were before.

You might be wondering who I am to be sharing all of this with you. In other words, what is it that qualifies me to be writing a book on living with Integrity, on becoming more "whole"? I can tell you with honesty and Integrity, nothing specifically. I am simply a spiritual being having a human experience, just like you.

What I am offering you however, is a glimpse at my own journey into living with FIERCE Integrity. In my story, you will see that I lived outside of my Integrity for much of my life. You will also see that living in this way created a lot of suffering in my life, suffering that I can now see was mostly unnecessary.

You will find that this book is divided into two parts. The first part of this book is my story. The funny thing is, I have always resisted telling this story. In fact, I spent most of my life denying that it even was my story. As you will read in the coming chapters, members of my family (my brothers in particular) have had to overcome some fairly significant health challenges over the past 30 years or so. These struggles have been ongoing and, in fact, continue to this very day. Until recently, it was my opinion that since I was the "healthy one" in my family, my story must not be worth telling.

In order for me to tell my story, something had to change in me. I have had to own my story as mine and see it as perfect. I have had to acknowledge that each and every thing that has ever "happened to me" was actually a gift. I have had to let go of any regrets that I may have been holding onto. I have had to release any desire for my life to be any different than it has been to this point. I have had to step into the belief that my story is worth telling.

Making these shifts has been unbelievably healing for me. Letting go of the past has allowed me to feel peaceful in the present. Forgiving myself for mistakes that I have made along the way has been important; forgiving others even more so. Writing this book has changed me. I feel more whole, more present, more peaceful than I have ever felt before.

I have chosen to share some of the details of my story with you, with the hope that some of the suffering you may be enduring can be eased. In my own journey, I have learned some strategies that have helped me to shift my perspective, to change my thoughts, to be present, and to live with Gratitude. Sharing these learnings with others is what the FIERCE Integrity Course is about.

Part Two of the book is the Course itself. You will find that my story continues to be infused throughout the lessons, offering insights and examples in order to help shed light on the concepts at hand.

How you use this course is up to you. I would encourage you to take what resonates with you and leave what doesn't. My intention for this course if to be of the Highest Divine Service for all those who engage themselves in its process. How deeply you choose to engage is fully in your hands. Before this book was finished, I elected to publish a shorter e-version of it online. In the e-version, which only deals with the Integrity of Thought, the tone of the material is quite different in that it is more casual, conversational even. It is administered over 21 days via e-mail messages. In the e-version I have invited participants to keep a journal, either written or electronic, to document thoughts and realizations throughout the course, and I would invite you to do the same. Many sections of the course also contain questions for you to answer. You can answer these questions in your head, or even connect with a group of supportive friends and go through this process together.

Know that by fully participating in this course, you are creating a space in your life for something new to come in. I believe that this course has the ability to help you create change in your life—radical transformation even—but only if you are open to change and willing to receive the gifts that it can bring.

To enroll in this free e-course please visit, WWW.FierceIntegrityBook.com and sign-up today

However you decide to tackle this project, know that it is the right way for you. In other words, it is Divinely Perfect! One option could be to start with the e-version. It is absolutely free and will get you thinking about the Integrity of your thoughts. Another option would be to read through the rest of this book and simply allow the words to sit with you, bringing a practice of awareness and contemplation to the course. Yet another option would be to keep a journal as you read through this course and take notes as you self-reflect and integrate some of the practices described.

Regardless of which option you choose, decide how long you would like to commit to this project for. How much time are you willing to dedicate to exploring this idea of stepping into your truth? A daily practice, involving a small amount of time, would be ideal— say 10 minutes per day. Of course, you can take more time if you wish. The point is that this is for you. This is your journey into living with Integrity. You get to choose what it looks like.

HERE ARE SOME QUESTIONS TO GET YOU STARTED:

What prompted you to pick up this book?

What are your intentions for this course?

What does Integrity mean to you?

What emotions or feelings does the word
FIERCE invoke within you?

AUTHOR'S NOTE

You may notice over the course of this text that certain liberties have been taken with respect to traditional capitalization rules. Given the fact that my approach to some of the topics described herein is quite spiritual in nature, capital letters are used to honor the Divine nature of certain words and/or concepts.

For instance, words such as Grace, Service, and even Integrity are capitalized throughout this text in order to convey their sacred qualities.

FOREWORD

One of the very first times I ever spoke with Maren, she shared with me her thoughts on perfection. It was in response to something I had written about giving up the need to be perfect. She didn't disagree, but she shared a take that resonates with me to this very day. Maren talked about how everything is perfect. No matter how it seems. No matter how it feels in the moment. Everything is perfect, just as it is. Whatever is in front of you provides perfect learning. Perfect opportunities. Perfect love. It is all perfect.

This doesn't come from a Pollyanna-like naiveté. Maren doesn't pretend everything is easy. She simply speaks with a deep trust in The Universe and in her path. She knows that whatever comes her way is a reflection of the profound and true wholeness that is the very core of all that is.

Maren doesn't just talk about FIERCE Integrity. She lives it. It's not an abstract idea where one thinks, "If only we could do it, life would be better." She does it. Finding the perfection in any moment is one of her many superpowers. She shows up fully, bringing a keen eye and a loving heart with her. It's not always an easy task to take what can be painful and view it as exactly what is needed, as not a form of punishment but as an act of love. When you read this book, you'll get to experience Maren's story. You'll get to see that it wasn't always neat and pretty. But it is always perfect. The perfection of it is one that is gleaned from Maren's inquisitive gaze. She looks at life with a gorgeous curiosity...even when what is happening is challenging. She opens her heart and mind to the possibilities that things will not just be ok but that they are ok.

When Maren started talking seriously about writing a book about FIERCE Integrity, I was downright giddy. This is a book that has the power to radically affect people's experiences. The teachings presented here can profoundly enhance your life by taking away the mind chatter of "not good enough" and replacing it with a tremendous sense of peace.

Living with FIERCE Integrity is not a simple task. It requires love. Trust. And a willingness to look deeply at what is present in your consciousness and to use it for your growth and upliftment. While not easy, it is full of power. From the vantage point of FIERCE Integrity, all of life is a gift. You can live that gift and enjoy a beautiful experience of freedom. This book creates a sacred and safe place where deep inquiry and powerful love is available. You are about to embark on a beautiful adventure. It will all be perfect.

Jo Anna Rothman

PART I

*My Journey into Living
with*

FIERCE *Integrity*

CHAPTER 1:

Two Small Babies

I had a fairly ordinary childhood. As far back as I can remember, I had friends, I did well in school, and I did well in sports (well, some of them, anyway). Generally, I was a pretty happy, healthy kid. My parents got a divorce when I was two, and my mom re-married when I was three. This was a bit unusual for this time period (the early '80s), but not shocking by any stretch of the imagination. I spent most of the time with my mom and stepdad and two weekends a month with my dad. The fact that this might not be the most "traditional" arrangement didn't even occur to me until I went to school and found out that most of the other children in my class (all but one) lived with their mom and dad.

I am told that I had a lively imagination as a child, and that I had a group of imaginary friends that I was rarely without. One of these friends in particular, "Baby Laura," took on a strong identity and role in my life (don't ask me about the baby part, I was almost a baby myself when I came up with these names). In fact, my mom relates a funny story about shopping with me and "Baby Laura." At the time, I was about two or two-and-a-half and it was my routine to sit on the very edge of my stroller so that Baby Laura could sit behind me. It was one of those umbrella strollers, flimsy things that they are, and I can only imagine how uncomfortable this precarious position would have been. My mom reports that I would sit like that for hours while she shopped. No matter how many times she would encourage me to sit back into the seat I would refuse, insisting that Baby Laura was sitting there. One day, as she was pushing me out to the car in the parking lot, she hit a bump with the stroller. I started screaming and crying telling her that Baby Laura had fallen out. As you might imagine, I was inconsolable and insisted that my mom find Baby Laura and put her back in the stroller. I smile at the thought of my mother running frantically around the parking lot, asking her toddler where this invisible being was so that she could scoop her up and bring her to safety!

My first half-brother was born in October of 1983. I was four at the time and very excited to become a big sister. I don't remember much about that time, just that my mother was very, very ill throughout her pregnancy, especially at the end. I also remember that my mom's mom came to stay with us (a rare event) and we made fresh raspberry pie, yum! When the baby finally came, I remember going to the hospital to see my mom and new brother. I put on my best dress and I was so excited! I was happy to have a baby brother but also sad that he couldn't come home right away. I didn't know it at the time, but this delay was unusual.

It turns out that Erik was born very premature. He was an extremely small baby, weighing only 2 pounds, 7 ounces. We didn't know it at the time, but things were only going to get far, far more complicated. He came home about seven weeks after he was born and we settled into life as a family of four.

I adjusted well (if I do say so myself) to my new role as a big sister. I was very attentive to the baby and cared for him a great deal. My parents did a great job helping me to adjust and I still felt loved and cared for.

Life rolled along smoothly until Erik was about twelve months old. Around this time, my mom and stepdad began noticing some signs and symptoms that something might be wrong with his vision.

After further investigation, their worst fears were confirmed: something was indeed very wrong. After performing an eye exam under anesthesia, it was determined that Erik had a retinal disease in his left eye. He was initially diagnosed with Coates Syndrome, a unilateral eye disease affecting the retinal cells at the back of the eye. Erik underwent numerous Cryotherapy treatments to try and stop the disease from progressing. This is a type of treatment where liquid nitrogen is inserted in through the pupil and touched to the diseased retinal cells, essentially burning them in order to try and destroy them. After each procedure, Erik's left eye would be swollen and sore. He had 15 of these treatments over the course of two and a half years.

By this time they had changed his diagnosis from Coates Syndrome to Atypical ROP, or Retinopathy of Prematurity. It was deemed to be atypical because it only affected the one eye and ROP is typically bilateral. By the age of four, his vision condition appeared to have stabilized. Despite all of the treatments that he had endured, Erik was left with only light perception in the affected eye. The good news was that his right eye remained healthy and seeing, which allowed him to function quite normally as a toddler.

Due to my young age, and maybe a silent desire to forget some of the more painful moments, I don't remember very much about this time period. One of my more vivid memories is the myriad of emotions that I felt after seeing Erik shortly after one of his early Cryotherapy treatments. His left eye was swollen shut, leaking fluid, and literally swollen to the size of a golf ball. What a grotesque and horrifying sight on such a sweet, adorable little toddler! As the mother of a young child, the memory of this sight churns my stomach even today. At the time I felt alarmed, scared, and extremely sad for my little brother.

Around that same time period, Erik and I were involved in an accident together, which sent him back to the hospital yet again. We were playing with an exercise bike at my grandma's house (even though we had been warned against doing so) and Erik's finger got caught in the chain of the bike as I was pedaling the wheels around and around. It was awful. The tip of his finger was severed by the machine and it was bleeding profusely. My parents were panicking and Erik was screaming. Understandably, they left for the emergency room in a huge rush, leaving me with my grandma to wait by the phone for an update. I remember sitting in the dark living room, crying and staring absentmindedly at the TV, feeling sick to my stomach. In my mind's eye, I can still see the look on my stepdad's face as he left the apartment. At the time I thought it was anger, rage even, directed at me. Now, looking back, I can see that it was probably a deep sense of fear.

As for me, I felt an overwhelming sense of shame. I remember wondering if Erik might die from the accident, but I was too afraid to voice my concerns. Finally, at about two in the morning, my parents arrived to pick me up and take me home. Erik was with them and he was okay! The doctors even managed to save the end of his finger. I was so very, very relieved.

Life sailed merrily along for the McConnell family for a couple of years. Both of my parents were schoolteachers, thus they enjoyed the same schedule as Erik and I. Now that Erik's vision condition had stabilized, he was a happy, healthy preschooler. Our family was very active, and my parents were heavily involved in the running community. My mom even ran a sub-three-hour marathon, earning second place in the Richmond, BC marathon! By the fall of 1986, my parents were ready to try for another baby and they became pregnant. The baby was due in the spring of 1987. My mom's pregnancy was fairly similar to her pregnancy with Erik, although she didn't become quite as ill as she had with him. Nevertheless, at around seven months gestation, the fetus' growth came to a screeching halt, and again my mom found herself delivering yet another premature baby via c-section.

Benjamin John McConnell came into the world on March 11, 1987, weighing only 3 pounds, 1 ounce. My mom and stepdad found themselves once again driving to and from the hospital visiting their newest addition in the NICU. Erik and I were cared for by family and friends while they were there, and a few weeks later, Ben finally came home.

We adjusted to our new family member, and he to us. I was almost eight by this time and once more, relished my role as big sister. I loved to hold the baby and help change his diapers. I was happy to have my new brother home and not at the hospital; however, I remember feeling a bit sad that my room got moved down into the basement. Actually, it is the first time I remember acting out about anything (although I am sure it wasn't the first time, and it certainly wasn't the last!). I can recall having a temper tantrum at the top of the stairs, fighting with my parents about my room being down there. I lost my balance and ended up falling down the first couple of stairs and onto the landing.

It was the first time that I became conscious of the thought that maybe I didn't quite fit with my family anymore. I remember feeling like an outsider looking in and not wanting to feel that way. I knew that it wasn't Ben's fault—he was only a baby! But I couldn't seem to change the way I felt, no matter how hard I tried.

It turns out that I didn't have long to dwell on these feelings because at exactly twelve months, Ben started to show signs and symptoms of vision loss as well and our whole world got turned upside down.

CHAPTER 2:

Ben and Erik's Journey

We know now that the premature births of both of my brothers were caused by a genetic syndrome. This syndrome caused the placenta to stop developing earlier than normal, thus resulting in the need to take the babies out prematurely. The first symptom of this syndrome, other than premature birth, was, of course, related to vision loss. Ben suffered the same retinal condition as Erik, only it progressed far more rapidly and affected both of his eyes. As Ben's vision deteriorated, he also developed severe Glaucoma, an extremely painful condition involving increased pressure inside of the eyes.

Ben had 31 eye operations over a span of 2 years in order to try and save his vision, most of which were done in Boston, Massachusetts. We lived just outside of Edmonton, Alberta, Canada, which is a long, long way from Boston. As a result, each surgery also involved extensive plane travel with a very young toddler who spent a lot of time in an unimaginable amount of pain.

On one of the Boston visits, my mom was traveling alone with Ben. They were coming home after an operation and the pressure in his eyes was even higher than usual. As you can well imagine, the plane travel only exacerbated his pain and he spent the entire flight crying, screaming and writhing in pain. Old enough to talk at the time, Ben's only request, that he repeated again and again, was, "TAKE OUT MY EYES.... TAKE OUT MY EYES!!!" My heart breaks just thinking about this painful time in our family's history.

Those two years were a very difficult time for my family. My most vivid memories are of Ben, curled up on the floor with his head in his hands, his body rocking back-and-forth, back-and-forth. He too had the golf-ball-sized eyelids and for some reason, I never did adjust to seeing them. They still had the same sickening effect on me. I remember my mom and dad having to restrain Ben in order to put drops into his eyes, my mom remaining her ever-calm self while my dad reacted in frustration and anger. I remember running and hiding in my room during these times, crying in my closet so that no one would see my tears.

There were good times too, though. Ben and I were very close and he loved to listen to music. My dad had a large CD collection (CDs were brand new at the time and they were all the rage!) and Ben and I would crank up the tunes and dance together. I would hold him on my hip and swing him around to the beats of UB40—Ben's favorite.

Erik and I were close too. We spent a lot of time together because our parents were away a lot tending to Ben. Erik and I would have sleepovers in each other's rooms, especially when Ben was really sick and we were afraid. He adored me and followed me everywhere, which I found mostly annoying but sometimes flattering. We played house and school for hours together.

When both boys would go to Boston, as they did occasionally, I would often stay with family friends so that I could still stay in a "routine." I remember not liking this very much and feeling really alone and isolated from my family. One morning when I was staying with some friends, I woke up with a mild form of Bell's Palsy—a form of facial paralysis. It was fairly mild (affecting mainly my mouth, which impacted my ability to speak and smile) but I didn't know what was happening and I was terrified!

It didn't take long for the Palsy to resolve itself, but my mom took me for a checkup with a neurologist just to be on the safe side. That day with my mom was one of the most memorable days that I ever had with her while I was growing up. I remember going for lunch, just the two of us, and I remember how "special" I felt. It is the first time I can recall that I felt jealous of all of the attention that my brothers were receiving—and at the same time I felt angry and ashamed that I would have a thought like that! Again, I forced this thought from my mind and went back to doing my best as a daughter and as a big sister.

Despite my parents' having done everything possible to try and save Ben's vision, he eventually needed to have both of his eyes removed, rendering him totally blind. So, by the age of four, Ben's health crisis was seemingly resolved, leaving him mercifully pain-free. He would start his new life as a preschooler completely without sight.

It was an adjustment for all of us. My parents, knowing little about raising a child who was blind, began to access the supports and services of the Canadian National Institute for the Blind (CNIB). Fueled by the desire to know more and the need to do right by her son, my mom enrolled in a Master's program in San Francisco. She received her Master's degree in Special Education with a focus on children who are blind or visually impaired. She went on to do her PhD in Educational Psychology and, later, my stepdad and I both completed our Master's degrees in the same field as well. It became my parents' passion to advocate for their son, and to educate themselves so that they could support him in the best way possible.

Currently, Ben is enrolled as a student at the University of Victoria Law School. He is in his second year. He completed his undergraduate degree at Carlton University in Ottawa, including a year abroad in Scotland. I would say, and I know that he would agree with me, that my parents' support has had a huge part to play in Ben's achievements thus far.

Today, as I write this, Ben is recovering at home, trying to fight his way back to health after yet another setback. There have been many over the years, almost too many to count, for him and Erik both.

After the initial vision problems in both boys, other medical symptoms began to appear. In Erik, the first of these symptoms was a severe bone condition affecting primarily his left hip. At the age of eight, Erik began to experience intense hip pain and began to hop everywhere on his right foot so that he wouldn't have to put any pressure on his left hip. My parents were away when this behavior first started, and they had hoped that it might resolve itself within a few weeks. When it didn't resolve, they took him into the doctor for further investigation.

What they discovered was alarming. The head of Erik's left femur had deteriorated so that it was no longer fitting into his hip socket. He was diagnosed with atypical Legg-Perthes disease, a vascular disorder where blood flow into the femur is diminished, thus creating the disintegration of bone. Erik was on the higher end of the expected age range, thus the "atypical" diagnosis. The treatment was to admit him into the hospital for an extended traction treatment. It was hoped that this would re-establish the blood flow to the leg and create healing.

This treatment didn't work at all. So, instead, the next course of treatment was physiotherapy. Over the next year, Erik had to endure manual manipulation treatments three times per week from a physiotherapist. This involved rotating the head of the femur around its full range of motion within the hip socket. Erik, still only eight years old at the time, found these treatments to be excruciating.

Despite the efforts of everyone involved, no progress was made. Further attempts were made to ease Erik's discomfort; casting his legs, an osteotomy, which involved cutting his pelvis in half, two hip fusions, and finally, years later, a hip replacement. Erik's medical team was extremely hesitant to perform a full hip replacement on such a young person, as he was only 20 years old at the time.

Unfortunately, even this treatment didn't seem to work and he had to undergo yet another hip surgery only a year later to revise the hip replacement.

From a young age, Erik has had to suffer with a level of chronic pain that for most people is unimaginable. He has explored many options in order to try and manage the pain, from pharmaceutical treatments to more holistic therapies such as acupuncture. Now 29, he has yet to find a treatment that is effective and he continues to struggle with pain, arthritis, and finding a suitable dose of medications.

What's more, during all of this, other symptoms began to appear as well. His eye condition returned when he was 19, resulting in the need to take out his left eye. In addition, he and Ben both began to mirror very serious medical symptoms that were seemingly unrelated as well as inexplicable.

Both Ben and Erik experienced portal hypertension, a condition that results in fluid collecting in the abdominal cavity. Ben was on a Rotary exchange to Brazil when his symptoms began and he had to be medically evacuated in order to have a liver bypass surgery when he was 17. Erik's liver bypass happened very shortly after, when he was 21.

Shortly after Erik's liver bypass, he started to have GI (gastrointestinal) symptoms as well. He was bleeding into his GI tract, and he began throwing up uncontrollably and was hospitalized yet again, this time for 200 days! More recently, Ben has experienced some of these GI symptoms as well, resulting in a large amount of blood loss and a stay in the ICU in the summer of 2012.

Ben and Erik also developed grand mal seizure activity. Ben has had three or four of these very serious seizures, two of which resulted in hospital stays. In 2009 he had one of these seizures while he was living in Ottawa and the medical team there had to induce him into a coma in order to stabilize him. It was discovered that both boys were having seizures due to intracranial deposits of calcium on the brain.

Related to the calcium deposits on the brain, it was determined that both boys have low bone density, called osteopenia. This condition is quite severe in Ben and it has resulted in many broken bones over the years. As a child, Ben broke his tibia while running in a track meet. This break was relatively minor and it healed quite well. His next break came when he was 17 and preparing for his Rotary exchange to Brazil. This time it was quite a bit more serious as he had broken some of the vertebrae in his back. Next, he broke his arm while out walking on the campus at Carlton University, and he broke his back again while working in Montreal when he was 19. During his recovery in the hospital from that particular incident, he developed a very severe bedsore which nearly took his life.

Despite all of his medical setbacks, Ben was bound and determined to continue to further his educational career. He was thrilled to be accepted into several law schools beginning in the fall of 2010 and set off hoping for a fresh start in Victoria, BC. Unfortunately, it wasn't to be. During his first semester he fell down some stairs and fractured his skull. Then, right at the beginning of his second term, he broke his arm again. This time the arm took a very long time to recover, and it was still not completely healed by the time Ben came home for the summer. Just as that semester ended, Ben fell and broke his femur, adding yet another setback from which he had to overcome.

And yet somehow, he did it. He returned to law school for his second year and mercifully enjoyed two semesters incident-free.

In July, 2012 he elected to travel to Texas to take part in a National Federation for the Blind (NFB) Conference. On the night before he was scheduled to fly back to Victoria, he fell and yet again broke his leg. Much like the first femur break, it was a very serious break that required surgery.

My parents were heartbroken and seemingly shattered. How much more could Ben's body take? How much more could our family endure?

My dad elected to fly to Dallas to once again help Ben begin his road to recovery. At first it seemed that things were "business as usual." Little did we know that yet another storm was brewing. While he was in the hospital recovering from surgery, doctors discovered fluid building around Ben's heart and lungs. With difficulty, the medical team managed to stabilize him enough to fly him home, but shortly after arriving home he was admitted to the local hospital to investigate further.

Ben stayed in the hospital for almost seven weeks, and several times during that period his life hung in the balance. No one was even talking about the femur that he had just broken. As more and more symptoms began to appear, low blood numbers, bleeding in the GI tract, difficulty breathing and, of course, the fluid building around his heart and lungs, his case was moved from specialty to specialty, trying to determine a cause. It made for a long and stressful summer. Finally, in late August, they managed to stabilize him. After this last medical struggle, Ben was able to move back home, where he is trying to recover and hopefully return to his life in Victoria this winter.

Taking all of this into account, we know that at the very least, Ben and Erik have likely not seen the last of their health concerns. All we know for certain at this point is that the boys have a rare genetic syndrome, one that is causing all of these seemingly unrelated health problems. And given the fact that their condition is so rare, their futures remain rather uncertain.

As far as appearances go, both boys are smaller than average in stature, especially Ben, and have extensive signs of premature aging. In fact, both Ben and Erik have totally grey, or even white hair. (But then again, so does their dad, so there might be a bit of "traditional" genetics at play there too!)

I jest a bit at my stepdad's expense, but in all seriousness, it has been a tremendously long and arduous journey, especially now, as Ben faces another extensive road to recovery. As ever, he is the picture of optimism and hope, and yet it is evident that this journey is wearing on him, wearing on all of us. Each time Ben is forced to claw his way back to health and wellness, it seems to take him just a little bit longer to recover.

As for my parents, I know that they too will get through this. They always do. Ben will most likely get back to Victoria, hopefully in time to start the winter semester. And my parents will return to living in the torn state between hope and fear. Proud of their son's tenacity and bravery, and yet forever worrying about the next phone call that could come at any moment, sending them back into yet another tumultuous storm. It is a difficult existence.

Realistically, I know that both of the boys will likely have a shorter-than-average lifespan. This is a difficult concept to grasp... knowing that they could pass away at any time. When I sit with this thought, I am always quick to remind myself that any of us could do the same. The truth is, none of us knows how much time we have left.

CHAPTER 3:

My Story Begins

As I shared with you in the Introduction, I am surprised that I find myself telling this story. When I sat down to write this book about FIERCE Integrity, I had no idea that the story needed to begin way back then. I realize now that all of those experiences that have shaped my family in fact have shaped me. They have brought me to where I am today, and for that, I am eternally grateful.

Thus far in the story, I haven't talked much about how these experiences have affected me. I have shared a bit about how they affected me as a young child, but not much beyond that. It might seem odd to have shared so much of my brothers' story here, but I feel that it is relevant.

What makes their story relevant to my story is the fact that my brothers' health concerns have been a fairly defining characteristic of our family. Both of my parents have truly devoted their lives to advocating for their sons. It was essential that they do so, especially for Ben. My parents' support and advocacy have been crucial in navigating both the education and the medical systems. I shudder to think of where those boys would have ended up if it wasn't for my parents' love, intelligence, perseverance, and dedication to their sons' health and well-being. Now, as a mother myself, I can see that it has been a true labour of love.

Given the fact that I was the oldest (and, let's be honest, given the fact that I was healthy) meant that I was often left to my own devices. I was expected to be quite responsible and independent from a very young age, and as a young child, I had no problem doing so.

I am told that I was an agreeable child. Easy to get along with, cooperative, respectful. I was always eager to please my parents, and I very rarely required punishment of any kind. Of course, there were the odd misdemeanors—throwing berries at the neighbours' house, squabbling with my brothers, not eating my vegetables—but that was about it.

All of this changed when I became a teenager. On the surface, everything still looked normal...better than normal, even. I achieved high grades, winning many academic awards, including student of the year in Grade 6. I was on the honor roll throughout junior high and high school. I participated in a wide variety of sports, activities, and clubs. I had a lot of friends and I was well-liked by adults and other kids alike. I even had perfect attendance for much of high school—a feat which I am still told is quite remarkable!

While I managed to make sure that everything looked great on the outside, on the inside my world was falling apart. As I entered puberty and my hormones kicked in, I transformed from a happy child into a moody, difficult teenager.

A part of me must have desired to continue to please my parents, which is why I think I managed to uphold the illusion that my life was on track, but on another level, my anger towards my family's situation began to simmer deep within.

The ongoing health difficulties that my brothers were experiencing began to take their toll. I began to resent the fact that my mom rarely came to any of my school or sporting events. I grew frustrated each time we met an acquaintance and they admitted that they "didn't even know that Ben and Erik had a sister." I even began to resent being the "healthy one."

As these resentments continued to build, I also began to question my parents' divorce, wondering why they split up so many years ago, and wishing they were still together. I would fantasize about how my life would be different, how our family could've been "normal" if my "real" parents had stayed together.

I was discussing this with a friend one day, and she surmised that it must have been because my mom and stepdad had had an affair. She told me that she had overheard her mother talking about this and told me that she was repeating what she had heard.

I remember feeling shocked and outraged at this possibility. I stewed and stewed about this for a long time, wondering if it could be true. I was afraid to ask, afraid to know the truth...but one day, I finally gathered the courage to ask my biological father why he and my mom had divorced.

"Why don't you ask your mother," was his simple reply, his face darkening at the thought.

It took me many months to finally gather the courage to ask my mom, but I finally did so.

Mirroring my discomfort, my mom replied, "I don't feel comfortable having this conversation with you. This is something that I can't discuss with you until you are older." Her face was ashen as she looked at me, her eyes pleading with me to let it go.

"How old?" I challenged. I was furious and disgusted with her. To me, she had just confirmed her infidelity by not offering me the truth. My mind reflected back on the conversation that I had had with my friend, and my anger spread like wildfire until it encompassed both my mom and my stepdad.

"How about when you are 18?" She replied gently. I barely heard her reply as I turned my back on her. I was 12 years old at the time.

This day was a defining day in my early adolescence. The assumption that I made that day became a truth in my life, one that I felt I couldn't share with anyone. Because I had accepted this assumption as fact, it changed everything in my life. It changed the way I saw my mom, and I began to treat her very poorly, punishing her and even hating her for what I perceived were her transgressions. I dwelled on the fact that she didn't spend enough time with us, that she was always working or at school, and that she never came to any of my events or games. As my teenage years went on, we grew farther and farther apart. As for my stepdad, I punished him even more severely. I defied him at almost every opportunity and openly told him on several occasions that he wasn't my "real" dad. I can still remember the look of pain on his face when I said these hurtful words. I began to spend more time with my biological dad, although by this time he had remarried and he and his wife had two young kids of their own.

In my early teens I became very aware of the feeling that I didn't belong in either one of my families, and I began to reach out to my friends and their families for support. I spent a great deal of time with my best friend's family, spending my lunch hours there, going there after school, and having as many sleepovers at their house as my parents would allow.

I also began to seek out the attention of boys during this time and consistently had a "boyfriend" from the age of 13 until...well, now, actually. (Although I think my husband would be less than thrilled about me calling him a boy!) By the time I started high school, I was in a "serious" relationship with a particular boy and dated him for about three years.

It is difficult to admit these things to myself, even today. I started drinking at a very young age; I was first drunk at about the age of 14. I started smoking cigarettes in high school, although I worked hard to keep this a secret from my parents and adults in general. I experimented with marijuana, although I never did really enjoy this drug. My behaviour was fairly promiscuous given my young age, and I entered into a sexual relationship at the young age of 15. I

MAREN HASSE

would sneak out often during the night to engage in these activities, I missed my curfew consistently, I attended parties without my parents' knowledge, and even hosted my own parties at their house while they were out of town. Throughout this time, I demonstrated very little respect for my parents, nor did I feel that it was owed to them.

I also demonstrated very little respect for myself, specifically for my body. Around the end of junior high, I began to feel very self-conscious in my own skin, covering up my stomach at every opportunity and not allowing anyone to touch it. I began to loathe that part of my body and could hardly even look at my stomach in the mirror. I began to see myself as ugly and fat. My solution when I felt this way was to purge my food. I didn't do this behaviour a tremendous amount, but deep down I knew that what I was doing was harmful. Reflecting back, I know that this behaviour helped me to feel more in control of my life at the time.

To some people, this is all going to sound like "normal" teenage behaviour. For others, it may sound a bit harsh. From my perspective, it is somewhere in the middle. I wasn't in extreme amounts of trouble—I didn't get into trouble with the law, I didn't get into hard drugs, and I didn't get an STD. In that regard, I guess I would consider myself lucky.

I often wonder what prevented me from going even further down the path of self-destruction. Looking back, I remember having a deep sense of knowing that what I was doing was hurtful to my parents, but that I also didn't want to push the boundary too far. I was aware of the fact that I wanted to have a successful future, believing at that time that I had what it took to get into medical school. I dreamed of the day when I would leave home forever, go to University in a different city, and move on with my life.

Ironically, it is because of my parents that I believed in this favorable outcome. My parents raised all three of us (myself, Ben, and Erik) to have high expectations and high standards for ourselves.

Despite my deviant, destructive, and no doubt incredibly frustrating behaviours as a teenager, my parents never stopped believing in me.

Unfortunately, things would get worse before they got better. My high school relationship evolved, or I guess I should say devolved, into a fairly dependent one. I spent all of my time with my boyfriend, allowing my own dreams, aspirations, and interests to fade away. I became intertwined within the dynamics of his family, and formed close bonds with them, especially his mother. As a result, I refused to see the mutual destructiveness of the relationship.

In the spring of 1997, my high school offered an open house for graduating students, giving them an opportunity to explore different post-secondary options. One of the visiting schools, Queens University, made an exceptional impression on me. I just knew that it was the school for me. I took the brochure home and pored over it every night before I went to bed, staring at the ivy-covered walls of the beautiful buildings and imagining myself walking across campus.

Willing this dream into reality, I spoke to a guidance counselor who informed me that it was quite a competitive school and that I would be just on the cusp of being admitted with my current average. I applied that day and continued to remain hopeful.

Later that day, I remember telling my boyfriend about my application. I was surprised by his reaction.

"You can't do this to me!" He practically shouted at me before he stormed out of the room. At the time he was enrolled in his first year at a local college, as he had graduated the year before.

I remember feeling so confused. I hadn't really thought about how this would affect him. I had just assumed that he would be happy for me and encourage me to follow my dreams. I was taken aback by his anger. I immediately went to him to try and discuss it further, but there would be no discussion. He was adamant that I not go, even if I were to get in.

My parents had a very different reaction when I told them. They were excited for me and we had a special dinner that night to celebrate. It was evident that my stepdad was quite alarmed at the prospect of the costs, but he managed to put those fears aside for the time being and demonstrate that he was genuinely happy for me.

The next few months rolled along in a blur as I scrambled to finish my high school courses. I was also vice president of the graduation committee, so I was very involved in planning the party that was fast approaching. It was a busy time.

During this time, I received a letter from Queens telling me that I had been conditionally accepted. They informed that I needed to achieve an 86% grade point average in order to attend and, should I do so, I would be enrolled to start school in September.

At first I was elated! But then I quickly remembered the reaction that my boyfriend had had and my elation was immediately replaced again with confusion.

"What should I do?" I wondered to myself.

I decided not to tell my parents about the letter until I had made a decision. In the meantime, I also applied to the local university and found out that I had been granted conditional acceptance to their program as well. Their grade point average requirement was much lower, so I knew that it was very likely that I would be attending university in the fall—I just wasn't sure which one.

The day of the graduation party came, and it was one of the happiest days of my young life. I felt like a princess that day. My parents had purchased me the most spectacular dress and paid for me to get my hair and nails done. Both sides of my family attended the event, although I made sure to seat them at different tables. Two of my grandmothers attended, as did Ben and Erik. My boyfriend came, and he and my parents were quite civil with each other—a rare event. By this point, my parents were having a difficult time being supportive of the relationship, as they could see some of the negative impacts it was having on my life. None of this seemed to matter anymore, and I was able to enjoy what felt to me like the perfect day.

A mere four weeks later, I was in a very different place. I woke up lying on the bathroom floor and saw that I had been bleeding, a lot. I can remember cleaning up the blood with a towel and dragging myself back into my bed where I lay there crying and crying. So much had changed in the past four weeks. I had found out that my boyfriend was cheating on me and I had broken up with him. He was still trying to make amends, but I wasn't ready to hear it. Prior to this discovery, I had made the decision not to go to Queens University but to go to the local university instead, all because of a boyfriend who wound up breaking my heart.

On top of the breakup, I was still trying to integrate some information that I had received on my eighteenth birthday. I never forgot my mom's promise to tell me the truth when I turned 18 and I knew that I needed to take her up on it. We went out to lunch that week in early June, and I remember feeling sick to my stomach knowing that I was going to have to ask the question again and hear her response. I wondered if my mom would have the courage to tell me the truth. It turns out that she did have the courage to tell me the truth—only it wasn't the truth that I had expected to hear.

I found out that day that the real reason my mom and dad divorced was because of him. He had been unfaithful. When I first heard those words, I immediately wanted to deny them, but then old memories flashed through my mind and I knew that my mom was telling me the truth.

"But if you didn't do anything wrong, why didn't you tell me when I asked way back then?" I asked her. Shock had quickly turned into anger, and I was already feeling guilty for all of those years when I had believed the opposite scenario to be true.

"I didn't want it to change the way you felt about your dad." She said honestly, quietly. Her words startled me. How could I have not seen this coming? Why would she want to protect him?

"But MOM, do you know what I thought? I thought it was you and Roy who cheated! All of this time I was angry at you for wrecking your marriage!" I remember feeling panicked at that point, thinking about all of the horrible things that I had done and said to her over the years.

My mom laughed out loud at my words. First out of shock, I think, but then, perhaps out of regret, as the realization of the choice she made back then began to sink in.

I thought back to that conversation as I lay crying in my bed. It was July and my mom and stepdad were away with my brothers on holiday and I was home alone for a few weeks. I continued to reflect on the previous two weeks: finishing my diploma exams, my boyfriend cheating on me, deciding to cut my dad completely out of my life without even having the courage to tell him why, and choosing not to leave home in the fall even though that is what I desperately wanted now more than anything.

I had a summer job (which I managed to somehow keep throughout all of this) but I spent most of my non-working hours lying in my bed crying. To make matters worse, my best friend seemed to be avoiding me. I felt completely and utterly alone as I tried to make sense of my life.

I went fumbling along like this...until one day I remember being seized by the most intense abdominal cramps that I have ever had. I had had problems like this in the past, and had been diagnosed with ovarian cysts, but it had never felt quite so intense before. I remember going into the bathroom, where I must have collapsed. Waking up, I saw that I had been bleeding, which both scared and bewildered me. I felt weak and sick to my stomach, but I managed to clean myself up get back into bed. At the time, I don't think that I was fully able to acknowledge what was likely happening, the thought of a miscarriage being far more than my 18-year-old-self could handle. Pushing this thought from my mind, I eventually managed to cry myself to sleep.

CHAPTER 4:

Seeking

My family went to church quite regularly while I was growing up. I really enjoyed going; I had a lot of friends there, and I especially liked the youth group meetings and trips when I got a bit older. When I was in high school, I voluntarily took confirmation classes and started reading the Bible before I went to bed each night. I also taught Sunday school for a short while. I played in the handbell choir and sang in the youth choir. I didn't feel particularly connected to God, but I believed strongly that "He" existed.

One day during my confirmation classes, I began to ask a lot of questions of the pastor. I vividly remember him admonishing me for doing so and briskly returning back to his lesson. That same day he informed me that I couldn't be confirmed by the church unless I had been baptized and therefore they would be baptizing me on Sunday before the confirmation service. My mom and stepdad had chosen to simply dedicate each of us to the church when we were younger so that we could make the decision to be baptized into the church when we were ready to make that decision for ourselves. I was greatly touched by this act of respect from my parents, even back then. And, although I liked going to church and enjoyed being a part of the church community, I wasn't certain that I was ready to be baptized yet, especially given the fact that I had so many unanswered questions! After class, I tried to explain my concerns to the pastor but again, my concerns were quickly dismissed.

I decided then and there to leave my church and I never did show up for my confirmation service. This experience left me hurt, angry, and confused about the nature of God and religion.

Leaving my church and turning away from God (at least the only God that I knew at the time) was a major turning point in my life. My feelings of separation were intensified by my perception that my whole life was falling apart. By the summer of 1997, I had isolated myself from both of my families, I was losing my best friend and I had no idea why, and my boyfriend of three years had been cheating on me. I didn't know where to turn.

Probably not surprisingly, I ended up allowing the boyfriend back into my life. I felt more a part of his family than either of my own families, and I decided that I could forgive him for making a mistake. My self-destructive behaviours—drinking, smoking, partying—only intensified, and now that I was an "adult," I rarely came home to spend the night. I started school in the fall and found myself disillusioned by the university system. I began to attend fewer and fewer classes and spent most of my spare time with my boyfriend. Not surprisingly, I almost failed out of my first year and was given a "Dean's vacation"—basically a letter where the university asks you not to come back for a one year period. This was in stark contrast to the 86% average that I had earned in high school, just one year previously!

Almost exactly one year later, I learned that, once again, my boyfriend was cheating on me. This time, I knew that I was finished and that I needed to move on, but I didn't know how. Two of my male friends, Trent and Chris*, were going to Europe in the fall and I basically invited myself along. I worked three jobs that summer in order to save enough money to go. The plan was to go for three months.

*name has been changed

To my surprise, my parents were actually excited for me. They expressed often that they were very concerned for me (and understandably so). They were especially concerned about my relationship with my boyfriend and saw this as an opportunity for me to get out of that relationship for once and for all. Even though we were broken up, I was having difficulty staying away from him, as I truly felt at the time that he was all I had.

I managed to succeed in saving enough money to go on the trip and my parents were very supportive. In fact, my stepdad wrote me a letter telling me how proud he was of me. I knew it was the first time in a long time that I had given him reason to feel this way.

Given the fact that I was only 19 at the time, and that it was the first time I had really travelled abroad other than a trip with my biological dad and his family to Australia when I was 13, going to Europe was a shock to the system. I found myself quite fearful to be out in the world without my parents and away from my boyfriend. For the first three weeks, I resigned myself to the fact that I would have to tag along with my two traveling companions, even though they rarely went to the places that I wanted to see. Chris* (one of the guys) and I began to fight regularly as I tried to voice my opinions about where we should go and what we should do. He had his own agenda, and rightfully so! It was me who was too afraid to go off on my own.

Finally, about three weeks into the trip, I realized that I needed to leave the boys. I had worked hard to get here and I knew that I wasn't taking full advantage of this opportunity.

We were in Amsterdam when I told the boys that I was leaving and I made my way to the train station to catch a night train back to Paris. I was terrified. I remember sitting on my backpack in the train station, feeling jumpy, worrying about all of the "bad things" that could happen to me out on my own. I was crying and writing in my journal when I heard a familiar voice.

I looked up and there was Trent. My heart dropped into my stomach and I knew then and there that my life was going to change forever.

CHAPTER 5:

Love and Marriage

I don't believe in accidents, or coincidences for that matter. I have a strong faith that everything happens for a reason. Today I am married to Trent. We have been together in some way, shape, or form since that night in Amsterdam back in 1998. It hasn't been an easy journey. We have had to grow up together. We have stretched and eased into our identities as adults, never being able to escape the other person's need to change and grow too.

We have a child together now, a son, and as of the time of this writing, he is three years old. Over the years we have had many more traveling adventures, which have taken us to Central America (we got married there in 2004), Southeast Asia, South America, and across the United States and Canada in a '71 Volkswagen van. However, none of these adventures have compared with the journey that we have had as parents.

To begin with, we were uncertain about the likelihood of us becoming parents in the first place. Early on in our relationship, we were forced to have a very honest conversation about my brothers' health condition, and whether or not we would choose to have children should it be determined that I was a carrier of the gene that caused their syndrome.

I decided to undergo genetic testing in my early 20s, shortly after having a late period and a pregnancy scare, and it was determined that it was unlikely that I was a carrier although they couldn't tell me for certain. I found this news unsettling, but I managed to push it from my mind. I wasn't sure at the time if I even wanted to become a mother.

Around this same time, I found out that I might have difficulty conceiving naturally as I continued to struggle with ovarian cysts. My doctor informed me that each time one of these cysts bursts, it causes scarring on the ovary, making it more difficult for the ovary to release an egg on its own. I was startled by this news and afraid to tell Trent, thinking that he might not want to marry me if he knew that I might not be able to have kids.

He was more than reassuring, but it wasn't the first time that I feared that he would leave me. I spent a great deal of time worrying that he would cheat on me—or worse, eventually leave me. This type of thinking drove Trent crazy, and he and I fought about it regularly.

Trent's influence in my life helped to turn around a lot of my unhealthy behaviours. I eventually quit smoking, I drank less, and I finally stopped the purging behaviour. However, I found myself flirting shamelessly with other men, finding myself desperately in need of the attention, and more than once, this got me into some difficult and even dangerous situations. Unfathomably, Trent managed to forgive me when I got myself into trouble, and I thank God every day that he was able to do so.

Somehow, we made it through our early 20s and began to plan our wedding. That first night on the train from Amsterdam to Paris we agreed that we would get married on a beach someday—and that is exactly what we did. We got married in Costa Rica on March 7, 2004, among the company of thirty family members and friends. Both sides of my family were in attendance, as were both sides of Trent's (his parents are divorced too).

It was one of the best days of our lives...and to think, it lasted a whole week! The day that everyone left, we both lay in the bed in our hotel room and held each other as we cried, sad that it was over. But we still had a three-month honeymoon to look forward to, so the tears didn't last that long!

One of the greatest gifts that Trent brought into my life was the ability to let my parents back into my life. For some reason, his presence and influence in my life has allowed me to reconnect with them in a way that I had never been able to do before. Today, they are our best friends. We see them almost daily and enjoy an incredibly close relationship with them.

I have also forgiven my biological father, although we didn't actually speak about any of this until just recently. One of the gifts that this project has brought into my life was the ability to step into my own FIERCE Integrity, giving me the motivation and the courage to talk openly with him. I now know that everything unfolded exactly as it needed to in order for me to grow into the person that I am today, and I hold my father in a state of esteem and Grace. After all, half of who I am is because of him, and we are eternally connected with one another.

Trent's and my early married life together was fairly innocuous compared with our dating life. We had great plans to travel the world together and teach English overseas, but ended up living back in a van in the mountains of Alberta instead. We moved out to Nordegg (in Alberta, Canada) between 2004-05 and lived and worked at an outdoor centre. It was there that we met a group of people who would change us both in ways that we never could have imagined.

We got into outdoor sports in a big way and camped, rock climbed, ice climbed, paddled, hiked, and summited mountains alongside our new friends: Darcie, Jody, J, Brent, Dave, Mike, Cheri, Rolf, Andy, Mo, Bridget, Amanda, Billy, Monte...over the years, this group has only increased in size and these people have become like family to us.

In January of 2006, Trent and I made the very difficult decision to leave Nordegg and move back to the Edmonton area. We were feeling like we needed to get "real jobs" and make some "real money" as we found ourselves entertaining the possibility of starting a family. Edmonton is three hours away from Nordegg (or from mountains of any kind) and we found this to be a very difficult adjustment. Thankfully, my parents still lived in the area and we found ourselves spending more and more time with them, escaping all together to recreate in the mountains as much as possible.

Trent eventually found a job in his chosen field of engineering and I took a job working as a teaching assistant in a classroom with students who have severe disabilities. I was actually handpicked for the job as several of the students in that classroom had visual impairments and the principal of the school knew of my family and offered me the job.

It was a good fit. In fact, it was such a good fit that I decided to enroll in the post-degree program at the university to take my Bachelors of Education degree. (I did eventually finish my first degree, majoring in Psychology.) I was also encouraged to apply for a Master's degree at Mount Saint Vincent University in Halifax, in their distance education program for Teachers of Students with Visual Impairments. I was accepted to both programs and found myself very, very busy with these endeavors over the next two years.

In July of 2007, my parents celebrated their 25th wedding anniversary. We held a party in Nordegg at the hostel there and surprised my mom. Our dear friend Brent, the manager of the hostel, helped us to pull it off. We filled the hostel with my parents' closest friends and family members. It was a great night.

That night, I can recall staying up very late with one of my parents' best friends, Dr. Allan Bailey. In addition to being my family doctor, he and I enjoy a great relationship and I feel like I can talk to him about anything. This particular night, I remember voicing my concerns about having children, wondering if I could have them— and what's more, how I would know when it was time. Having three children of his own, he looked at me wistfully and took his time before he replied, "You just know. One day you might wake up and think, 'I have to have a baby this minute,' or, you might not. Either way, it will be what it needs to be."

Satisfied with his answer, I went back to staring into the fire, allowing a comfortable silence to settle between us.

Over the next few months, I reflected a few times on our conversation and wondered if perhaps I would be one of those women who would never really want kids. I rationalized this by reflecting on all of the difficulties that my parents have experienced with their boys, and considered that it might be best if I didn't ever have a baby.

A short while later, Trent and I were in Chile, sitting on the patio in the sunshine, enjoying our breakfast while overlooking the ocean from the condo we were staying in. I looked down at the words that I had just written in my journal.

I want to have a baby. It is all I can think about...

I wondered if now might be the time to tell him.

"Trent?"

"Uh huh?" He answered, distracted by the view.

"I think I want to have a baby."

His surprise was evident by the look on his face as he got up to get us some more coffee. He didn't reply for a long time. This is usually his way.

"Ok. Well, I need to think about it."

"Ok. I won't bug you about it. But you should know that I really want this and I am ready right now." I knew that it would be hard for me to not bring this up with him again and again, but also recognized that I needed to keep my word.

His silence told me that it was, in fact, okay and we both went back to staring out at the ocean.

A few weeks later we were back at home and back into our routine. I was entering the second year of both of the university programs I was enrolled in, and I didn't have time to think about much else!

Other than starting myself on a prenatal vitamin, I didn't dwell too much on my desire to get pregnant. Around this same time I had a regularly scheduled visit with my female family doctor. I told her about my plans to possibly get pregnant and asked her if there was anything else that I should know before doing so. She checked over my chart and shrugged,

"Other than the history of cysts, which we have discussed before, you don't have a history of miscarriages or any of the risk factors that would indicate that we have any reason to be concerned." She looked up expectantly at me, thinking that I would be happy with this reply and bring my checkup to a close.

A memory from eleven years ago flashed across my mind.

"Well, I'm not sure if I have a history of miscarriage or not." I said quietly.

"Excuse me?" my doctor said, closing her laptop and giving me a look of surprise mixed with genuine concern. "That's not in your chart."

"I know. I didn't tell anyone. I'm not even sure if I had one or not." I felt my face turn crimson with shame.

I told her my story about falling unconscious on the bathroom floor and waking up in a pool of blood.

"Hmmm..." she said, "You're right, that doesn't sound like a burst cyst—but we have no way of knowing for sure. Did you take a pregnancy test?"

I blushed an even deeper shade of red, if that's even possible, and shook my head, unable to speak.

Seeing the discomfort that is written all over my face, she put her hand on my knee.

"Listen, I don't think that you have any reason to worry here. You are a young, healthy woman and I can't see any reason why you shouldn't try and get pregnant. Whether you had a miscarriage or not, there is nothing to indicate that you would have one now."

I allowed her words to sink in and I began to relax, feeling the relief that comes from unburdening oneself of a secret that is finally revealed.

Despite the reassurances from my doctor, I was careful to not get my hopes up. Not only was I conscious of all of the unknowns that I was facing with respect to my fertility, but I was also very uncertain about how long Trent would take to arrive at the same place I was, and if he would even be able to do so.

You can imagine my surprise when a short time later, in February, 2008 he turned to me and out of the blue, said simply,

"If you still want to try and have a baby, I think I'm ready."

I was elated. Not wanting him to change his mind or to over-think things too much, I immediately took him up on his offer.

Knowing that the odds were against me on so many levels, I refused to let myself believe that it could have happened on our first try. Even when, three days later, I knew something was different, my mind couldn't accept the possibility that I was pregnant. By the time two weeks had gone by, the signs and symptoms that I was indeed carrying a baby were irrefutable, and yet I still insisted on taking four home pregnancy tests, finding it incredulous that it had been so easy for us to conceive.

This was not what I had expected. Even though I knew that this is what I had wanted, I found my new reality to be quite an adjustment.

Mostly, I was excited about the happy news, and hopeful about all of the possibilities that the future held. But from underneath my joy emerged something completely baffling: a deep sense of fear.

I booked an appointment with my doctor and insisted on subjecting myself to yet another pregnancy test. (Thankfully these tests are noninvasive in nature and as simple as peeing in a cup!) My doctor was a bit confused about why I was there; after all, I was only four weeks along, and he let me know that they usually don't start seeing prenatal patients until they are entering into their second trimester, at three months.

I knew what at least part of my fears were about, but I was having difficulty giving voice to these thoughts. My doctor did it for me.

"Really, our main concern in the first trimester is miscarriage, and there isn't much that we can do other than wait and see what happens. Given your age and your health, you shouldn't have anything to worry about. If it happens it happens, but you don't present with any of the risk factors that would indicate that we have any reason to be concerned."

I didn't feel the need to re-hash the mystery incident from so long ago, and was happy to finally leave it in the past. I made my appointment for two months from then, and left the office.

About two weeks later, I was hard at work in the school where I was doing my teaching practicum. I had offered to teach a free yoga class to any of the interested teachers in the mornings before school started, and since my doctor had given me the go-ahead to continue with my regular activities I never gave it another thought.

One morning, after teaching my yoga session, I found that I wasn't feeling great, and was experiencing a lot of cramping throughout my belly. I excused myself from the classroom and made my way to the staff washroom.

Hesitantly, I checked my underwear, fearing, expecting the worst...and my fears were confirmed as I saw spots of blood marking my underwear. I sat down feeling paralyzed, frozen with fear.

"What am I going to do?" I thought frantically, "My supervising teacher doesn't even know that I am pregnant. Why is this happening to me? What should I do?" My mind was racing, trying to figure out how I was going to handle the situation.

In the end, I ended up telling the mentor teacher about the pregnancy and the bleeding. She was very supportive and encouraged me to go straight home and rest.

On my way home I phoned my doctor's office and asked if there was anything that I needed to do. They were very sympathetic and emphasized that there was nothing I could do but rest. They also told me that I might not even necessarily be miscarrying and that I would just have to wait and see.

A few days came and went. Thankfully, it was the weekend and I was temporarily relieved of my daily responsibilities at the school. The bleeding stopped, and I wondered if it would start again. I was afraid to do anything physical and spent most of the weekend on the couch or in bed.

My parents were away during this time and didn't even know I was pregnant. I spoke with my doctor's office again on Monday and they advised me to continue with my usual daily activities but suggested that I ease up on the yoga. I asked my mentor teacher to accompany me to tell the principal that I could no longer offer the class.

Of course he was understanding, and congratulated me on the happy news, smiling broadly at me.

It occurred to me then that two people other than Trent and I knew about our pregnancy—and that these were people I barely knew! All of I sudden I became desperate to tell my parents, and worried about how disappointed they would be if they should hear the news from someone else!

That night we made plans to tell them as soon as they got back from their trip. As the week went on, I allowed myself to begin to feel excited about the pregnancy again. I made my parents a special card and bought a bottle of non-alcoholic champagne. The week seemed to drag on and on as I waited for Friday night to arrive.

When it finally arrived, I could barely contain my excitement. I casually slid the news-bearing card across the counter, willing them to open it.

I was in their home office with my dad when I heard a huge cheer from the kitchen. I knew that my mom had opened and read the card.

My dad looked up at me, eyeing me curiously.

"What was that about?" he asked.

"You'll see. Come on, let's go find out." I said over my shoulder, as I practically floated towards the kitchen.

My mom had tears in her eyes as she rushed over to hug me.

"Really? Is it really true?" She asked me, her voice filled with hope and expectation. My dad was struggling to catch up, picking up the card from the counter. "Is what true?"

A huge belly laugh erupted from him as he finally learned the news, and he beamed at me and Trent.

We opened the champagne and celebrated into the night as we chatted excitedly, and I filled them in on what they had missed so far—for the first time allowing myself to truly relish my feelings of hope for the future.

CHAPTER 6:

Expecting and the Unexpected

I am a planner, at least with some things. I also like to be prepared, which usually means that I carry around a massive purse, along with several other bags almost everywhere I go. From the moment I found out that I was pregnant, I immediately felt the urge to read and learn as much as I could on the subject, and toted along at least one of the five pregnancy books that I had purchased everywhere I went.

Much to my shock and delight, my belly was quick to develop, and by the time I was ten weeks along, I had a rather large protrusion from my midsection, making it impossible to keep our secret any longer. We started telling our friends and family members, along with the rest of the staff at my school. Of course, given my appearance, most people were not surprised to hear the news and many of them commented on how large my belly was for so early in my pregnancy.

Of course, I began to fret about this, wondering if something could be amiss, and scoured my books for a clue as to what could be happening. One night I awoke in the middle of the night and I couldn't sleep. I was staying with my mom as the boys had gone down to Moab, Utah, for a mountain biking trip. I tried in vain to put myself back to sleep, but to no avail. I was feeling hungry, and, giggling to myself, I got up to get myself a snack and brought it back to bed, finding this unusual urge and behaviour amusing. I settled in to read one of my books, trying to look up a reason why my belly might be bigger than most at only 10 weeks.

I flipped to a page from the appendix and stared dumbly at the page. Twins.

"You have got to be kidding me," I thought to myself.

I closed the book, turned off the light and snuggled back down under the covers, staring into the dark. I had lost my appetite.

In the morning, I gingerly shared the possibility with my mom. She did a great job of reassuring me to stay calm and encouraged me to make a doctor's appointment on Monday morning. I did so and got an appointment scheduled for later that week.

The week dragged on as I waited for my appointment, trying to distract myself with thoughts unrelated to babies, bellies and the like. When my appointment finally arrived, I sheepishly admitted my concern about the possibility of carrying twins to my doctor, aware of the fact that I had now been here for two visits prior to the three-month mark.

He admitted that he thought this possibility unlikely but didn't dismiss it completely, and suggested that we schedule an early ultrasound just to be safe.

"An ultrasound?!" I was excited by the idea of finally getting to see my baby (or babies) and know for certain that he/she/they were okay. I agreed readily to the procedure and went downstairs to make my appointment at the imaging clinic.

Unfortunately, on the day of the ultrasound appointment, my husband was called out of town on business at the last minute, but my parents offered to come with me, excited to see an image of their first grandchild!

I went in by myself at first and laid stock still as the technician conducted the exam, I found myself holding my breath and willing everything to be alright. After what seemed like an eternity, she finally turned to me and asked me if I would like to see my baby.

"Just one?" I asked cautiously, bracing myself for the answer.

"Just one," she confirmed as she left the room briefly to go and get my parents.

The baby didn't look like much at that first ultrasound. I mostly just remember its little frog-like legs kicking up into the space of my womb. I remember being filled with a deep sense of relief as we all laughed and gazed happily at the screen together, relishing the gift of seeing my son for the first time.

A short time later, I completed my teaching practicum and all of the requirements for my Master's degree. I was grateful that this hectic time in my life was finally coming to a close. I was eagerly anticipating having five months to focus solely on growing a perfect, healthy baby...my baby!

My first few days of freedom were quite blissful. I slept a lot, ate a lot, and generally enjoyed a lot of lazing about. I also took full advantage of the abundance of free time that existed within my day-to-day reality by doing prenatal-themed meditations. I even tried my hand at prenatal-themed art, making every effort to connect with my baby and my pregnancy as much as possible.

As the summer wore on, I found myself having more and more difficulty filling up the days and, much to my chagrin, I began to notice that an old feeling was beginning to creep into the back of my mind: fear. With increasing frequency, I would catch myself entertaining negative, even dark thoughts about all of the things that could go wrong with the pregnancy or be wrong with the baby. Desperate for confirmation that all was still well, I never missed a doctor's appointment, each time sighing with deep relief when I got to hear the now familiar sound of the fetal heartbeat. My relief always seemed to be short-lived and I began to once again count down the days until my next doctor's appointment. I believed that once the baby started moving more and more that this would be reassuring for me...and yet, when I did start to feel the baby's kicks inside my belly, it only became another source of worry.

"Is the baby kicking too much? Is the baby kicking too little? The baby hasn't moved much this morning, I wonder if everything is okay." The voice in my head was relentless.

Even though I tried to find a balance between what I knew were somewhat irrational fears and valid fears, I became obsessive about everything that could harm a developing fetus. I was afraid to exert myself too strenuously, I was afraid to lift anything, I was fearful over what I ate and drank...each new fear became more gripping than the last. I felt powerless in the face of it all.

Despite the war that was being waged in my mind, my body continued to stay the course. It seemed to know exactly what to do, and thankfully, it just did it. Looking back, the amount of anxiety that I subjected myself to is almost laughable given that I had such a healthy, normal pregnancy.

At the 20-week ultrasound, everything was found to be normal, as was expected based on the first ultrasound and all the prenatal exams. They told me that the baby was in a breech position—meaning that its head was up and its bum down but that it would almost certainly flip to the reverse, several times even, before it got too big and it was too late for it to do so. I had a brief conversation with my doctor about what they do if a baby is still breech at term (scheduled C-section), but he again reassured me that given the fact that it was still so early in my pregnancy, I had nothing to worry about.

I had a deep sense of knowing at that time that the baby wouldn't turn. I don't know how I knew, but I did. I began to do more and more mediations and visualizations preparing myself for a natural birth, trying to bury this knowledge that I held deep within me. At the time, it was very important to me to have a natural birth. I wouldn't have been able to articulate it then, but I know now that I held a belief that if I didn't deliver my baby naturally that I wasn't a fit mother. That I wasn't truly a woman.

In hindsight, the advantage of having a baby who is breech in utero was that I was scheduled for two more ultrasounds through the second half of the pregnancy—something which they wouldn't have had to do otherwise. Like the prenatal exams at the doctor's office, I relished these times to connect with my baby in a more tangible way, and the brief interlude that they provided me from my suffocating anxiety.

Much to my chagrin but not my surprise, the baby never did change from its breech position and I was scheduled to have a C-section on Monday, November 3, 2008.

Chephren Dax Hasse made his entrance into the world on a drizzly, gray morning. As I would expect happens to most parents, I found that giving birth was a life-changing event (even though it was not a natural birth as I'd hoped). I can still remember the first time I laid eyes on him and the overwhelming sense of love and gratitude that I felt. He was perfect. A perfect, healthy baby. I was so proud and relieved.

Because of the C-section, I had to stay in the hospital for the first four days, and required quite a bit of support from Trent. From the beginning, I struggled with breastfeeding, but believed that it would only be a matter of time before Chephren and I sorted it out. By the time I was scheduled to be released from the hospital and take the baby home, I was starting to feel a bit panicked about the breastfeeding situation, as it hadn't improved thus far; in fact, it was only getting worse.

When we got into the car to come home, I forced myself to push my fears aside and try to enjoy the momentous occasion. We stopped for a coffee on the way home and I repeatedly peered over my shoulder into the backseat at our beautiful, sleeping miracle. When we arrived home, I took Chephren from room to room, whispering softly in his ear as I toured him around our house, his house. I remember feeling content and happy.

He soon woke up for a feeding, and I sat down on the couch trying to find a comfortable position in which to breastfeed him. It had started to become more and more painful each time I tried feeding him in the hospital—but the amount of pain that I experienced on this particular occasion took my breath away. Tears sprang to my eyes as I tried to relax into the feeding, but the reality of my situation—home with a brand new baby that I wasn't sure I could feed—hit me, and I started to wail. Wrenching sobs began to emerge from deep within my belly as I gave in to all of the emotions that I was feeling. Our dog, unsure of what was happening began to howl back at me. I felt defeated. Humiliated. I couldn't comprehend how something that was so natural, breastfeeding, could be so difficult, so painful. It led me to again question not only my identity as a woman, but my identity as a mother.

"What kind of mother can't breastfeed her baby?" I thought to myself.

I had been seen briefly by a breastfeeding specialist prior to leaving the hospital in order to make sure everything appeared to be in order with the "mechanics" of the situation. I was told that they couldn't see any reason why I would be having trouble and dismissed my concerns.

The days went on like this. Each feeding was a physically and emotionally draining experience. In addition, and not unlike most new mothers, I found myself becoming more and more fatigued as my body tried to heal from giving birth and adjust to my new sleeping routine (or lack of it!). Chephren turned out to be one of those babies who would only sleep when he was held, and I found myself sleeping on the couch each night with him on my chest.

Prior to becoming a parent, my husband and I had a lot of opinions about parents and parenting practices. I would often judge other people's parenting choices and we would discuss the practices that we wished to implement when we had our chance as parents. Ha! So much of what we had discussed went out the window as we adjusted to life with our son.

One of the parenting beliefs that I held prior to giving birth was about sleeping. I believed that it was important for a baby to learn to sleep in its own bed right from an early age, day one if possible. I believed that this was important for not only the baby's safety but for the mom and dad's well-being as well. I am not justifying it; it is simply what I believed to be true at the time. When Chephren came home with us, I found myself giving in to his every need and request. I couldn't bear listening to his little newborn cry even for one second, and I would do everything in my power to help him become calm again. If he wanted to sleep on my chest at night, he got it! My needs really didn't matter. Given the fact that I desperately needed to sleep as well, I'd say it was actually a win-win situation. Looking back on these early days and weeks with Chephren, I wouldn't say that we were thriving, but simply surviving.

After four weeks of couch-sleeping, Trent and I began to really miss each other. He talked often about how much he missed feeling close to me, and it became harder and harder to part at bedtime. I started to feel lonely and sad at night and would often cry myself to sleep. I told myself that it was partly due to the hormones and partly because I was so overtired. I forced myself to bring my focus back onto the beautiful baby sleeping on my chest and I would calm down, breathing in his magnificent scent.

After a few too many nights like this though, I knew that we needed a change, and we transitioned Chephren to a low cradle next to my bed. I found that I could soothe him by laying my hand on his chest and talking or singing to him softly. Eventually, he became used to his new arrangement and I started to get a lot more sleep.

The breastfeeding battle was another story. At his 10-day checkup, my doctor told me that Chephren was becoming jaundiced and had lost too much weight since his birth. He told me that he was in danger of being a failure-to-thrive baby if something didn't change for him soon. When he asked me about the breastfeeding, my eyes filled with tears and my cheeks flushed crimson with shame.

My doctor insisted that I consider switching Chephren to a bottle and supplementing my breast milk with formula. I was so disappointed in myself, but I knew that it was the right thing to do. He gave me a bunch of information about formula feeding and I went directly downstairs to rent a breast pumping machine and buy both bottles and formula. For two weeks, I pumped as much as I could, but each time I was able to get less and less breast milk until I eventually found that I was pumping for the entire 2-3 hours between feeds!

I also continued to struggle with my breasts; by this point, I had mastitis (a breast infection) in both of my breasts and I was in agony. I remember getting into the shower one night and giving into my feelings. I cried and cried, feeling guilty that I couldn't give my son what I believed he needed the most at the time. I felt like I had already failed him as a mother and he was still so young! How was I ever going to get through this? I started to have thoughts that maybe I didn't deserve him, and that maybe he would've been better off with another mother—but I pushed these thoughts from my mind each time I held him close and looked into his beautiful, perfect face. I was in awe of the amount of love I felt for that tiny being.

The first three months were an absolute blur. I was finally healed from my operation; it took a bit longer than expected because I insisted on returning to my strenuous activity of choice, running, earlier than was recommended. Running had always been something that helped me to cope with stress and anxiety, and in those early months as a new mother, I really missed the feeling of serenity that it brought me. I also returned to yoga and found myself working on a contract with Alberta Education, an unexpected gift from the Universe. I knew that it was a great opportunity, as this type of contract would allow me to work from home and spend as much as time as possible with my son. After watching my mom simultaneously work a full-time job and complete graduate degrees during my childhood, I knew that I wanted to try and stay home with my son, especially while he was so young.

When he was really little, I found that working from home was fairly easy because the baby slept so much. As he grew older, I managed to find a young woman to come into my home one day a week and take care of him. I paid her well and felt good about the fact that I was only a few steps away should my son need me for anything.

I also enjoyed the freedom and flexibility that this type of work provided. Trent and I had such an extensive traveling history prior to having Chephren that I found myself already itching to go on a trip. The fact that our son would fly free until he was two held particular appeal to me, and I decided to meet my sister and stepmother in Nevada for a one week holiday when Chephren was five months old. I was nervous about flying alone with him, but as it turns out, he did wonderfully on the journey down South.

For the first part of our trip, Chephren and I had a great time. My stepmom and sister are avid golfers, so while they golfed every day Chephren and I managed to explore the area, visiting many national and state parks and reveling in the beautiful scenery and weather that the desert has to offer in mid-March.

About mid-way through the trip, Chephren woke me up in the night. He had a raging fever and blood in his diaper. I was terrified! My stepmom was very supportive and helpful, running to the store to get baby Tylenol, a thermometer, and anything else she could think of that would help. I didn't sleep the rest of the night, watching and waiting to see what would happen with my son.

In the morning, not much had changed; he was still spiking a high fever and I was having trouble controlling it with the Tylenol. After making several calls home to talk to Trent, my mom and dad, and our family doctor, I decided to bring him into the emergency department at the nearby hospital. I was petrified that something was really wrong, and I could not resist my need for reassurance from the medical staff at the hospital.

Thankfully, Chephren was fine (it turns out that he was battling the flu), but this incident was the first of many over the next few years where I would find myself overreacting and giving in to my deep, dark fear of losing my son. What had haunted me throughout my pregnancy followed me right into motherhood.

Living in this increasing state of fear began to really affect me physically. I stopped sleeping, I became lethargic, I had trouble making decisions, and I lost the desire to see my friends or do any of the activities that I loved. It all came to a head when one night, lying awake for yet another night, I indulged a fantasy that had been brewing in the back of my mind. I began to plan my escape. I told myself that Chephren and Trent would be so much happier without me, and I began to figure out where I would go. Perhaps to India where I would sit in an Ashram. Losing myself in this train of thoughts, I drifted into the most blissful, peaceful sleep that I had had in months.

I awoke the next morning to my beautiful, babbling, happy baby and I knew that I wouldn't leave, that I couldn't leave. How I loved that little man! I felt an overwhelming sense of guilt for even considering the possibility of walking away from him, and I knew right then that I needed to get help.

The next week, back in my doctor's office, I confessed my shameful feelings to my doctor. I told him about the building physical and emotional symptoms that I was experiencing, and he diagnosed me with postpartum depression (PPD). I knew that this diagnosis was coming, and yet I found myself feeling devastated. I was so disgusted with myself for allowing it to get to this point. With a very heavy heart, I agreed to the prescribed treatment, drug therapy, and went home to somehow break the news to my family.

It was easy to tell Trent, and I think on some level, he was relieved at the prospect of things getting better. Telling my parents was another story. My whole adult life I had tried to protect them from my problems, telling myself that I couldn't have anything wrong with me because of how sick my brothers were/are. Even so, I wasn't prepared for my mom's reaction: "You can't have depression! I don't think that you do; you don't look depressed or act depressed." All of a sudden I found myself in a position where I was feeling like I had to justify my diagnosis and try to explain why I had asked for help. Again, I felt shame for the situation and blamed myself for not being stronger.

In hindsight, my mom's reaction is understandable. I have always hidden my true feelings very well. I am the type of person who will tell you something shocking in order to avoid telling you what lies a layer or two beneath. I have repeatedly "put myself out there" in order to substitute the need to be truly vulnerable. Admitting that I needed help was the most vulnerable thing that I had ever done in my life. Another reason why my mom may have reacted the way she did is because, on some level, the story in her head was that if I was depressed, then she hadn't done enough to support me. This is not at all true, of course, but you can see how her mind may have taken her down that road.

Either way, being vulnerable and speaking my truth not only allowed me to get the help that I desperately needed, but it allowed my relationships with my friends and family to be transformed. Until this point in my life, I had been trying to be the daughter, the sister, the friend, the mother, and the wife that I believed my family wanted me to be. In order to do this, I thought I needed to change myself in some way. When you hold a belief like this, it seems true. I truly thought that the real me wasn't enough. Admitting that I had depression, standing in this truth, was an act of authentic Integrity (I call it FIERCE Integrity). In doing so, I was able to free myself of this limiting belief, essentially transforming my perceived reality. In essence, it was only me who was placing conditions on the love I was able to receive. It may seem paradoxical, but owning one of my perceived imperfections (my depression), allowed me to better see my true and underlying perfection. It allowed me to see that who I really am, my true self, is worth loving. This led me to the discovery that who I really am is so much better than who I think I should be. This profound realization has become integral to the work that I do. As a coach and facilitator, seeing this truth about myself has allowed me to see this same truth in others. So many people do not realize their own Divine perfection; they don't see how beautiful they are (both inside and out). They are afraid to stand in their own light. I feel so very fortunate that the work I do now allows me to help guide people towards realizing this truth for themselves.

CHAPTER 7:

The Rules of Engagement

My depression was diagnosed in July of 2009. Now, sitting here three years later, my life has been completely transformed. Making the decision to ask for help, to finally admit that I couldn't do this on my own, to be truly vulnerable, was the impetus for this change.

Prior to that day in my doctor's office, I had spent a great deal of time (arguably, all of my time) living from a place outside of my Integrity. Essentially, I was living in a state of denial. Denial about who I really was. About Who I Am. The voice in my head, my ego voice, had ruled all, and it had me believing that the real me, should I have chosen to express myself in my true form, was never enough, nor would it ever be enough. I lived in a state of fear. I was afraid to be rejected for being who I really am, and therefore I engaged in a great deal of pretending to be someone else, changing like a chameleon from situation to situation. I was someone different in each moment, playing the part that I believed I needed to play to be loved, to be accepted. After engaging in that behaviour throughout most of life, I wasn't even certain who the real me was.

It hasn't been an easy road to recovery and self-discovery, but it has been a rewarding one. The first year after my depression was diagnosed was the hardest. It took a lot of time for the medication to "kick in" and along the way I had to endure a lot of side effects. To make matters worse, I really resented needing the medication, and saw it as evidence that I wasn't a good mother and that I was a weak human being. As such, I was open and willing to explore other treatment options. I joined a local support group for other mothers who have PPD (though I did not have a good experience with this, so I quit after two visits). I saw yet another psychologist (I saw a few while I was growing up and dealing with my brothers' illness). I looked into Ayurvedic and holistic health practices, and I learned as much as I could about treating depression with diet and lifestyle practices.

Interestingly, the most effective part of my treatment plan, which was self-prescribed, was to be open and honest with my friends and family members about my depression. Continuing to be vulnerable with those who loved me allowed me to continue to live from my place of truth. Every time I admitted to someone that I was suffering and they didn't turn and run, it served to reaffirm to me that I was worth loving, that I was enough!

I wouldn't have been able to see it back then, but continuing to live from my place of truth began to seep into other areas of my life. I began to see other realms in which I was living outside of my Integrity, and I began to muster the courage and the energy to change them. One example of this was when, back in January of 2010, I committed to "Living with Less" for one year. What this meant for me at the time was halting most of my consumption practices for a full year. I blogged about the project, calling it "MareBare Necessities," and went along for the ride as I watched the project grow and change as it evolved throughout the year.

The project took me to places where I hadn't quite expected (for instance, I eventually gave up shampoo, gave up my clothes dryer, taught myself to sew, and made all of my own crackers), but the reward was truly a life-changing experience. I loved the challenges that it presented to me, the opportunity that it provided for me to write, and the connections with like-minded people that it brought into my life. I also relished the opportunity to continually question

MAREN HASSE

my beliefs, and to repeatedly ask myself what would have Integrity for me. It is the first time in my life that I had done so on a consistent basis, and I found it extremely liberating.

By the end of the one-year period, we had saved $40,000, an impressive fcat, but this financial advantage turned out to be minute when compared with the life lessons that I had gleaned.

Shortly after the project ended, my life would take yet another unexpected turn. I went away for a girls' weekend with a close friend, Darcie, her cousin, and her sister. Leading up to this weekend, I had been on a spiritual journey. After my falling out with the church in my late teens, I found myself seeking for spirituality in other traditions, taking courses in Buddhism and reading many books on the subject. I also became interested in yoga and completed my teacher training program in 2005 on a one-month retreat in Mexico. My understanding of meditation and spirituality only deepened on that trip, and I was treated to my first direct experience with God or Source. I had no way of integrating it back then, but it was enough of a taste of the infinite to keep me moving forward on my spiritual journey.

When I made the decision to be vulnerable with my friends, it allowed my friendships with several people to deepen, and one of these was with my friend Darcie. Darcie and I have been friends for most of our lives, since we were 12 years old, but we were able to connect on a deeper level when we discovered that we share a mutual interest in spirituality. In fact, we began to feel cosmically connected as we found that we both shared a sense of urgency to get onto our spiritual paths.

My weekend away with Darcie and the girls marks the defining "new beginning" of my spiritual journey. Throughout my 20s I had had quite a few "experiences"—but on one particular weekend in February of 2011, I feel like I woke up to a new reality.

From that point on, I began to experience the world differently. I became much more aware and attuned to the fact that there were two voices within me, a voice from my head (my ego voice) and a voice from my heart or soul (my intuition, or a deep sense of knowing). Through meditation practice, I found myself being much more willing to trust and act on this inner knowing, and a short time later I took myself off of the anti-depressant medication.

I need to be clear about something here. I am not suggesting that anti-depressants are "wrong" or "bad." They certainly helped me to right the ship when I didn't have anywhere else to turn. I was able to stabilize my depression through the help of drug therapy, and during this stabilization period, I was able to learn some other coping tools and strategies to help me from falling back into a depression.

Thanks to these coping strategies and tools, I have managed to stay off of anti-depressant medication since March of 2011. For me, while I found that the medication helped me to avoid feeling my lows, it also prevented me from feeling my highs. As someone who tends to feel things at a volume of 10 (out of 10!), the anti-depressants definitely helped me to "turn down the volume," but I also felt that they were preventing me from hearing my inner voice clearly.

In hindsight, they were doing exactly that. I have come to understand that emotional reactions (I call it button pushing) are actually strong messages from our soul. Every time you react emotionally to something or someone in your environment, you are being presented with an opportunity. You cannot choose what happens to you in life, but you can choose how you react to it. In each moment then, we get to choose whether or not we want to live from our centre (our heart) or give into the story in our minds (the ego). Choosing to live from our heart is to choose to heal whatever it was that was taking you out of alignment with your soul, with your inner knowing.

A few months after weaning myself from the anti-depressants, I was presented with the greatest opportunity for healing that I had ever been presented with to date: the death of a dear friend.

On May 2, 2011, three of my closest friends, members of my "Nordegg family," were out recreating together in the mountains. They had gone out for a late-season ski touring adventure in the icefields of our Alberta Rocky Mountains. Unexpectedly, one of the group, Brent, fell into a crevasse while skiing up the glacier, and he was not wearing a rope. His two skiing companions immediately initiated a rescue; however, Brent had fallen too deep into the crevasse to be reached by a rope. One of the skiers immediately skied out to notify Parks Canada so that they could initiate a larger-scale rescue. Brent was still alive in the crevasse, and they were unsure whether or not he had sustained life-threatening injuries. In addition, time is of the essence when you are initiating a crevasse rescue, due to the risk of hypothermia to the victim.

Several factors worked against the rescue team that day, one of them being a storm that began brewing as they arrived on scene. They had difficulty landing the helicopter in the building weather conditions. They did eventually manage to do so and continue the rescue efforts—but despite the superior efforts and knowledge of both his skiing companions and the rescue team, they were not able to rescue Brent before he succumbed to hypothermia, and he was pronounced deceased upon reaching the hospital in Edmonton.

The next days and weeks were a blur as our group of friends gathered in Nordegg over several weekends to mourn our friend and celebrate his life. Our two friends who were involved in the incident stayed with us in the initial days afterwards, and seeing them process their grief was particularly difficult.

It was the first time in my adult life that the world felt truly out of control, that the Universe didn't make sense anymore. In hindsight, I can see now that this event threw me radically from my centre, and I began to operate from a very ego-minded place.

My ego-mind is a very judgmental place, and I found myself judging my emotions, judging the situation, and judging the actions of others continuously. At the time, the voice sounded something like:

"I should feel more than I do right now."

"I have to be strong for this other person right now; I can't give in to my true feelings."

"I should feel less than I do right now; I feel as though my heart might explode."

"Why isn't Trent with me right now; why isn't he showing his emotions?"

"I need to be with my friends right now, but I feel guilty about leaving my son at home."

"Why Brent? Why now? This is so unfair! Why did this happen? Why, Why, WHY?!"

The voice in my head was relentless. I felt uncomfortable in every situation, with every emotion. So displaced from everything that I had thought I had known to be true. I was in a tailspin.

One day, my mom was pressing me for details, asking me to be truly vulnerable about my feelings, and I managed to convey enough about what was happening in my mind that she became inspired. She brought forth some wisdom that essentially picked me up from the crazy road I was on in my mind and brought me home into my centre. We now call this Divinely inspired wisdom "The Rules of Engagement."

I am not totally sure how The Rules of Engagement evolved from that conversation with my mom, but I shared those words of wisdom with Darcie (also a close friend of Brent's) and we built on them as we navigated through the grieving process.

Here they are, in their basic form:

The Rules of Engagement

Rule #1: It is what it is

This rule points to the fact that we are at the mercy of the Universe. As humans, we tend to engage in all kinds of behaviours that give us a sense of control—but at the end of the day, we are not in control, because control is an illusion. When things are going our way, this is an easy concept to grasp. We are happy to rest in the knowledge that "it is what it is" because all feels well in our lives. In fact, when things are good, we rarely even enter into this thought pattern.

When "bad" things happen, though (that is to say things that we perceive as bad) we react in a totally different way. In our state of emotional turmoil or anguish, we often begin to question the situation, demanding, aching to know WHY. "Why did this happen?" This is ever-so-often the case when someone dies, especially if that person is a young, healthy, vibrant individual.

I have entertained these thoughts myself, many times. "Why did this happen to me?" "Why did this happen to my brothers?" It took losing one of my close friends to finally surrender this need to know. I don't know why Brent died that day. I can't know. Do I think that there was some higher purpose or plan at work that fateful day? Maybe, but I can't be certain. In other words, I had to accept that it is what it is. I can't change the fact that it happened; I can only be present to each moment and be open to the experiences in my life. Losing Brent was one of these experiences. It was an event that touched a lot of people's lives and became the impetus for transformation in our community.

Rule #2: Allow and don't judge

This rule evolved specifically from managing the grieving process as a community, as a family. Each person needed the time and space to grieve Brent's death in his or her own unique way, free from judgment. Before integrating this rule into my own life,

I found myself being really critical of the way others were handling the situation. My husband, for instance, chose to handle his grief by removing himself from the situation, almost completely. He elected to work down the road, continuing to build our house in Nordegg, rather than come to the Center for Outdoor Education where our friends had come to gather. I couldn't fathom why he would want to isolate himself from us, and I found myself taking it personally.

This concept of letting go of our judgments of others first crept into my consciousness during the grieving process but now plays a central role in living with FIERCE Integrity.

RULE #3: LOOK AFTER SELF

This rule has to do with the idea that when we look after ourselves, when we "fill our cups," we are better able to serve others. This has to do with taking care of ourselves on not only a physical level but on a mental/emotional level as well. I would even take it one step further and say that we must engage in spiritual self-care as well. While physical self-care consists of a pretty standard list of things to consider (proper rest, proper nutrition, daily exercise, etc.), the activities that support emotional and spiritual health are going to look different for everyone. The main thing here is to know what your own personal tools are. This concept also made its way into the Integrity Course as well.

RULE #4: BLINK AND BREATHE

This rule is all about being in the present moment...yet another tool we'll explore in the Integrity Course. It is about finding your centre when your world feels like it is collapsing into chaos. It is about taking life one moment at a time and not allowing your thoughts to drag your energy into worrying about the future or dwelling in the past. It is about focusing all of your psychic energy on the task at hand. Brent was an avid outdoor enthusiast: a backcountry skier, a rock climber, an ice climber. He loved the thrill of adventure, the rush of adrenaline. I was fortunate to have had many adventures with Brent in the outdoors, and he was a skilled teacher about the importance of staying present during these activities. When you are engaging in activities that require a lot of your attention and focus, combined with a certain level of risk, the present is a great place to be!

RULE #5: LIVE AUTHENTICALLY... EVEN IF IT'S UNCOMFORTABLE

(and it will be uncomfortable)

One of the greatest gifts that I was able to receive from Brent was the example that he set for me. Brent was one of the most authentic individuals that I have had the Grace of knowing. He lived from the place of his truth unlike anyone that I had ever seen before. He was quirky, eccentric, and it was evident that he rarely, if ever, worried about what anyone thought about him. That is not to say that he was egocentric or arrogant; the opposite couldn't be truer. He lived with a sense of humility that continues to inspire me to this day. Living from this place of truth, this place of Integrity, is not an easy thing to do. It is a courageous act that requires a tremendous amount of stamina and a deep connection with your heart-centre. Because of his ability to live from this place, he has made it possible for others to do the same. In his passing, he essentially left a standing invitation for all those who knew him to find their own place of truth, and to live from that place.

Oh Brent, how I miss your mischievous grin and that twinkle in your eye! Thank you so much for being in my life and allowing me to receive these miraculous and transformational gifts from you!

Brent's passing awakened me to the fact that I was not fully living my truth. I began to see that the life that I had been living was not my own. In each relationship and situation, I found myself changing to try and better suit what it was that I thought each person or situation needed or wanted from me. I was living completely outside of my Integrity. I was living a lie.

The realization that I was not living a life of Integrity was shocking to me at first. If you would have asked me prior to Brent's death if I believed that I had Integrity, my answer would have been a resounding YES! When the truth of the situation emerged into my consciousness, it was difficult to look at, and difficult to accept.

At first, I didn't know where this new realization was going to take me. I just knew that I was on a train to somewhere different and that I couldn't get off, not even if I tried. Something had shifted inside of me. I had been forever changed.

Over the next few months, I watched my life transform dramatically. At first, it felt as though my marriage would fall apart, as I finally began to give voice to the cracks that had been there all along. It was in this ability to shine light on our marriage that we were able to see it for what it really was. We were able to readily identify what was working and what wasn't, and with our new-found awareness, we were able to change what wasn't working. Six months later, we emerged as a completely different couple. We now hold a level of respect for one another that we had never been able to achieve before. We have been able to authentically and unconditionally love each other for who we are instead of who we wish the other person could be. It has been a miraculous transformation in a relatively short period of time.

My relationship with my son and motherhood in general has continued to shift and change. I would be lying if I said that I no longer had the fear of losing my son; however, I manage this fear now by continually bringing my focus back to the present moment. He is here now. He is a gift in my life today, and one that I am worthy and deserving of.

My relationship with my family has continued to evolve as well. It is fairly typical for our family of origin to keep us tied up in the past, and I have been no exception to this, especially as it pertained to my relationship with Trent. Recently however, I am finding myself more and more able to let the past be in the past, and rest my focus in the present moment with each of my family members. Given the recent resurgence of Ben's health difficulties, the reality of potentially shortened lifespans for both of my brothers really began to sink in. This kind of thinking has the potential to be crazy-making—dragging me into fear for the future or guilt and regrets about the past. I know beyond a shadow of a doubt that I need to stay present now more than ever before. It feels like the ultimate test, and most days, I feel up to the challenge.

Importantly, I have learned to discern when I am operating from my heart-centre or when I have followed my mind down a "wormhole" in time, either past or future. I find myself more and more able to stay in the present moment for longer periods, and I am getting much more adept at bringing myself back to my centre when I stray. For this I am grateful—and yet I know that it is not me that is responsible.

I say this because living from my centre is to live in a state of Grace. It is to become a vessel or a channel in order to allow the Divine nature of who you really are to flow through you. Living with Integrity is to live from this place of Grace inside of you.

CHAPTER 8:

My Journey into FIERCE Integrity

In the preface, I described the shamanic journey I experienced on May 2, 2012. It is my belief that Brent's soul was with me in that cave and that his presence was indeed an answer to my prayer. In April of 2012, I had started working with an intuitive coach. There is no better way to describe it than to say that I felt called to work with this coach—and in doing so, I was able to step into my own role as a coach, writer, and facilitator. Even though I knew that I was on the right path spiritually, my mind insisted on loudly voicing all of the reasons why I was not able to do this work. I feel fortunate that I have learned not to listen exclusively to the voice in my head and, as such, I have been able to continue to follow my heart down this road.

Part of what I feel called to do is write. I have always been interested in writing, and from a very young age I wrote stories, narratives, articles, and speeches. In my early adult life, I didn't feel compelled to share any of my stories, although I kept writing them, losing myself in the creative process. It wasn't until the MareBare Necessities blog and the Living with Less challenge that I began to write more publicly. For me, it served as an accountability tool and it worked! I was able to finish the project and I blogged about it the whole time. When the project ended, I didn't feel as compelled to write on the blog. I found myself questioning what to do with it;

whether or not to take it down or build on it in some way. I received a lot of e-mail asking me to continue writing, and I was surprised that people, some of them strangers, were so interested in what I had to say.

When I got honest with myself, asking myself "What's in the way?" I identified that I was afraid. I was afraid to write from the heart. When the project was running, I always had a "topic" to back me up, to keep me on track. Without that crutch in place, I was going to have to simply sit down, tap in to what I call the "flow" (heart-centre) and write. It felt scary. Vulnerable.

When Brent died, it was the impetus that I needed to embrace this fear and move past it. After all, if he could live (and die) from such a place of vulnerability and authenticity, I could certainly write from that same place, couldn't I?

I would love to report that upon making that decision, I just sat down and did it. This wasn't the case for me; I first had to spend some time nurturing my inner artist, and connecting with that inner voice. After about six months of doing this type of inner work, and making gradual changes to my writing along the way, I was finally ready to step fully into the light. I wrote an article for the blog in November 2011 about change. It was the first time that I felt 100% vulnerable, that I found myself posting from a place of 100% Integrity. Here is what I wrote that day:

> *I think that I've talked about this before...in fact, I know that I did. I wrote about people changing (and argued that they do, and that I did). Now I am going to write about the other side of the coin, so-to-speak, the part where we, humans, society, (or what have you) aren't always open to change. In fact, that is putting it lightly. People (or so it would appear to me) generally abhor change.*

> *But why? What is it about change that makes us crazy? I changed my blog formatting, for example (and I will totally admit that it is making me uncomfortable). It is something*

simple and in the big scheme of things not at all important, and yet, discomfort, uncertainty, and maybe even some anxiety are creeping in. Now magnify that by about a billion and we are getting to the heart of it. Change in people's lives is a HUGE deal. Change at work, change at home, change in your relationships, change in the economy, change on a GLOBAL scale. And I hate to break it to you, but the changes are just going to keep coming, faster and more 'furious' than ever before.

So how do we cope with all of this change? Well, the first thing I am going to say is that to resist change is futile (more about futility, I know!) Resisting isn't going to stop the inevitable and in fact will only delay your acceptance of it, leaving you 'behind the 8 ball' as you attempt to reconcile the change(s) once you have finally accepted them.

If we aren't resisting change, what are we doing then? The feelings I described above are real...they exist and I would even say they are warranted. I am not saying 'don't feel that way' or 'suck it up, princess' or 'would you like some cheese to go with that whine?' (or any other silly cliché for that matter). What I am trying to get at is: how do we acknowledge those feelings and then move beyond them?

This is the part where I have you waiting on the edge of your seat, right? You are fully expecting me to have the answer and share it with you, yes?

The truth is, I am still trying to sort it out myself. I feel like saying, 'All that I know for sure is that I don't know' (!). Not helpful, I know. But I guess it begins with awareness and 'shedding light' on the situation.

Here is what I am proposing...the next time that you see changes on the horizon, I would encourage you to follow these principles:

1.   Don't hit the panic button! And I know that you know exactly what I'm talking about! Another way to think of this

step is to BLINK AND BREATHE! Pause, delay...in other words do whatever it takes to 'stall' your instinctive reaction (it's just your ego rearing its ugly head). Stalling will allow you the time to get into your heart instead—where your intuition lives...

2. *Notice, shine the light on, bring awareness to what is coming up for you: what emotions are you feeling and where you feel them in your body. Now here is the tricky part... You actually need to feel them...breathe into them. A wise friend of mine helped me to see that during this step walking outside and being in nature helps. The physical movement actually helps to move those emotions through and out of the body. Sounds simple (and obvious) but it works! Even better if you can do this with a great friend who will listen to you but not enable you to stay in those feelings for too long.*

3. *Now that you have acknowledged and released the feelings and emotions associated with the 'change' that you are fearing, you should feel lighter...like there is now some 'space' in the body/mind to look at the situation in a new way. Now you are ready to allow the change...and yes, even accept it.*

   The winds of change are eternally blowing, and yes, the wind might even be picking up in your corner of the world. The choice is yours; continue to resist, or figure out how to integrate, accept, and maybe even thrive on change.

Looking back on this post now, it doesn't feel all that vulnerable—but for me, at the time, it felt like I was essentially outing myself from the "spiritual closet" in a very public way. It made me uncomfortable, and yet, I knew it needed doing.

The Universe has been kind enough to respond with an affirmation that my ego so desperately needed: my reading audience quadrupled after that post, and it is still the most read post on my blog to this day. This statistic serves as a great reminder to keep pushing myself out of my comfort zone.

There have been many vulnerable posts since that day, all seemingly preparing me for something bigger. I didn't know what that "something bigger" was, and I found myself asking for Divine guidance. Sitting in meditation that day in May, on the anniversary of Brent's death, my prayer was answered.

When I got home from the meditation that night, and the realization of all of this sank in, at first I felt afraid. My ego ever so dutifully gave voice to all of my fears:

"What the heck is FIERCE Integrity?"

"Why FIERCE, what the heck is that about?"

"What am I supposed to say?"

"Who the heck am I to write about this?"

"Where do I start?"

"What if I screw this up?"

And on, and on, and on...

Much like I did when I posted my article on change, I pushed that voice aside and allowed my heart to lead the way. I managed to take my ego out of the equation as the first edition of the FIERCE Integrity project literally came pouring out of me in the days to come. Four days after the meditation and my encounter with Brent's message, I had a 20,000 word document. It came that easily, that effortlessly.

What emerged from the ether and onto the page was not what I had expected. The initial document came through in the format of a course, a course on living with FIERCE Integrity.

On May 31, 2011, I had written the following quotation in my journal:

Watch your thoughts; they become words

Watch your words; they become actions

Watch your actions; they become habits

Watch your habits; they become character

Watch your character; it becomes your destiny

*~Author unknown ***

**In researching this quote on-line it would seem that there is some controversy as to its origin... Regardless of its origin, I am thankful for these words!

I had no way of knowing it then, but this quote was to become central to the FIERCE Integrity Project. In fact, the first version of the course was broken down into three parts: Integrity of Thought, Integrity of Word, and Integrity of Action. In thinking about the word "Integrity," a lot of people would categorize it as a character trait, and I would tend to agree. Going back to this quote then, it would appear that what we think, say, and do all contribute to living with Integrity.

I was surprised and delighted to find that so many of my own learnings over the past few years fit so beautifully into these categories. Again, I felt overwhelmed with gratitude for the Divine guidance which I had received, and amazed at the beautiful synchronicity of it all.

What I have come to understand is that I spent most of my life living outside of my Integrity. What I mean by this is I was living my life without a lot of awareness or self-reflection. I held strongly onto my beliefs without ever taking the time to question those beliefs or wonder where they came from. I had very little connection with my heart-centre, allowing the voice in my head to run my life. I didn't notice how those thoughts were creating my entire reality around me. I was living a life filled with assumptions and judgments—towards myself and towards others.

A defining moment in my story was admitting to myself and finally to my family and friends that I was depressed. It was the first time that I truly questioned the voice in my head (it was saying, "You can't have anything wrong with you") and decided to act against it. I trusted my intuition instead. My gut was telling me that something was wrong, really wrong, and that I needed help. Taking that first step into my Integrity, into the light, has allowed me to significantly alter my life.

I should tell you that from an outsider's perspective, my life might not look that different. I still have two brothers who struggle with illness, I am still married with a young child, and I still participate in many of the same activities that I always have. From another's point of view, it may appear as though nothing has changed. What has changed radically is me; my perspectives, the way I feel in the world, the way in which I choose to react to each and every situation that comes my way, it's all different. Sure, old patterns re-emerge, necessitating some inevitable re-learning, but generally, I am happy. Grateful. Peaceful. Whole.

This is not to say that I am done with my journey—far from it, I suspect! I hold the belief that if you are still here when you wake up in the morning, you're not done learning the lessons that your soul desires to learn. I still get "squeezed" by people and situations, but I consciously choose to try to shift my perspective when I feel like life is going sideways. I still find myself knocked out of my centre, and yet I know that I will find my way back to this peaceful place that lies within me.

FIERCE Integrity is a course that is intended to help you find your centre and to live from that place as much as possible. When you live from a place of authentic truth, you are living from your heart-centre. You are no longer being governed entirely by your ego-mind, but by the knowledge that lies within your soul. Within all of our souls. We are all connected, we are all one. I have come to understand that it is our hearts that connect us to one another. When we live from our heart-centre, we begin to see the world as

Divinely perfect. We begin to see that all is as it should be. We let go of judgment and start allowing. We invite peace into our lives.

Part of my own journey into living with FIERCE Integrity has been to take an honest look into my past, and I have shared much of that with you here. When my family heard what I was up to in writing this book, they showed signs of hesitation, signs of alarm, as they weren't exactly certain that disclosing such personal details of my life, of our lives, was necessary or of value, and for a long time, I would have agreed.

The way in which I have told this story is different than it would have been had I told it in the past. The events would have been the same, but the voice would have been very different. I have told you this story from a heart-centered place. From a place of Integrity. From a place of authentic truth.

Had I told this story earlier in my life, it would have sounded a lot different because I would have told it from an ego-minded point of view. I would have sounded more like a victim, it would have had more of a "poor me" sound to it, or a "poor them."

That has certainly not been my intention; in fact, I couldn't even tell you the story from that place if I tried. The simple fact is, I don't feel that way anymore. I'm not sad about my past, and I don't feel like a victim. The truth is, I feel grateful. Grateful for each and every experience that I have had...even the hard ones. Actually, especially the hard ones.

Have I made mistakes? Absolutely, many of them. I am not saying that I am without flaws, please don't misunderstand. What I am trying to say is that those mistakes are perfect. I have had the opportunity to learn from them. I have had the opportunity to forgive myself for all of my mistakes and in the process I have had to learn to love myself in spite of them. I have had to do the same thing for each and every person in my life as well. I have had to let go of judgment and authentically forgive. I have had to let a lot of things go.

Am I perfect? Yes and no! Even I have to laugh at the seeming audacity of this statement. What I mean by this is that my soul, the part of me that lives in my heart-centre, is Divinely perfect, and when I live from that place of truth, I live with Integrity and I live this perfection. When I fall out of this place of truth and fall out of my Integrity (it still happens, often!) I make mistakes, I get squeezed, I find myself needing to forgive myself or someone in my life, yet again. And so it goes.

As I said earlier, if I am fortunate enough to wake up in the morning, I know that I am going to have more opportunities to choose how I live.

Even as I sit here writing this from my heart-centre, from my place of truth, there remains a part of me that questions these truths. When I wrote this part of the book, my brother Ben was lying in a bed of the Intensive Care Unit at the local hospital, quite literally fighting for his life.

In my heart and soul I know that it is all good...it is all perfect. And yet my rational mind, the voice in my head, is protesting this situation. Watching someone that I love suffer so greatly and sitting with the fact that he could quite possibly pass away at any time feels like torture. The medical challenges that both of my brothers face are difficult for everyone involved, and I find that these challenges repeatedly pick me up and throw me out of my centre. I start to entertain all of the fears and anxieties in my mind and I react physically and emotionally.

No one said the lessons would be easy, and that is why you must be FIERCE. At first I wasn't sure why the word FIERCE had to be a part of it, let alone why it needed to be so boldly emphasized. It is because in order to live from our hearts we must be bold, we must be FIERCE, and we must be relentless in our quest to do so.

When I think about my journey into my own Integrity and heart-centered awareness, I feel as though I have had to take on elements of the Archetype of Warrior. As a yoga instructor, I have spent a lot of time thinking about the word "Warrior" as it is one of the core poses in the hatha yoga asana practice. To me, being a warrior is to be FIERCE and focused, but I feel that there is also a softer side. A warrior is often quietly determined, and at peace behind the mask that they wear. A warrior must live strictly in the present moment, for there is no room for thoughts of the past or present as they would simply cloud the mind and possibly jeopardize the task at hand.

As I have mentioned before, the e-version of this course starts with the Integrity of Thought and getting at that "voice in your head." My own journey into living with FIERCE Integrity actually started from looking at my actions, and then my words, and finally my thoughts. I have shared that a defining moment of truth for me was admitting to my depression. Another defining moment for me came five months later when I launched the MareBare Necessities blog and challenged myself to a year of Living with Less.

After admitting that I needed help, I started to become aware of many other areas in my life where I wasn't living from a place of Integrity. I started to feel like a hypocrite, noticing where the beliefs or values that I held so strongly weren't lining up with my actions. This feeling of hypocrisy became increasingly uncomfortable until it became unbearable, and I impulsively committed myself to the MareBare project.

MareBare Necessities: Living with Less came about in January of 2010...a few weeks after the Christmas season ended. Over time, Christmas had evolved into a holiday that "pushed my buttons." This feeling had probably arisen from a few life experiences (one of them being my fallout with my church) but I also think it is strongly tied to my traveling experiences. Throughout our 20s, Trent and I had the opportunity to travel to many areas of the world, including Southeast Asia, Central America and South America. One of the ways in which traveling affected us significantly was that it changed how we saw consumption and material wealth. Seeing so many people around the world living in poverty made us not only truly come to appreciate how fortunate we are as Canadians, but it also forced us to examine our own use of resources. As a nation and as a culture, we are involved in a tremendous amount of consumption and, worse than that, an overwhelming amount of waste. In our country, the excess of each of these things is especially evident at Christmas.

Becoming a parent only intensified my feelings of shame and disgust with respect to our excess. I felt strongly about changing our lifestyle habits but I didn't know how. After cringing my way through yet another present-filled Christmas, I knew that I had had enough.

At the time, I didn't know where the MareBare journey would lead me. Ultimately, it led me here, to you, to this project. The year of Living with Less is part of my story; it is part of what led me to living with FIERCE Integrity. It forced me to sit with and answer questions that I had never had the courage to answer before.

Know that I don't expect anyone to do a year of non-consumption. That is simply what worked for me. As much as it was a year of non-consumption, it was a year of self-reflection, and **THAT IS SOMETHING THAT I AM ASKING YOU TO ENGAGE IN**. Stepping onto the path of living your truth is just that, a journey. A journey towards shining light on the dark, a journey towards asking those hard questions and sitting quietly as you wait for a Divine truth to come forward.

When I started my journey, I hadn't yet considered the notion that my thoughts created my words and that my words created my actions. All I knew at the time was that my actions and the choices that I was making didn't "feel good." I now know that this "feeling" that I was experiencing, this discomfort, arose because I was in a state of cognitive dissonance. This is a fancy term for saying that what is reflected in our behaviours doesn't match what is happening in our mind. To put it even more simply, we think one way but act another. When we act in opposition to our beliefs or our thoughts, it creates disequilibrium in our state of mind, a state of extreme discomfort, and our mind will work very hard to regain a state of equilibrium or ease.

It can do this in two ways. The first option is that your mind can subconsciously identify the belief in which you are acting in opposition to, and change that belief accordingly. In my consumption example, it would look something like this: I go out and spend a whole bunch of money on Christmas presents. I wind up feeling very uncomfortable with this act because it goes in opposition to what I say that I believe. I tell myself that "I really didn't spend that much money" and "It was all stuff that we needed." As I recall, this is exactly how it played out for me in December of 2009.

In this situation, however, my mind wasn't able to fully "buy in" to the lie that I tried to tell it. Inside, I knew that it wasn't true and I couldn't avoid this truth any longer. For me, this resulted in a need to change the behaviour to one that fell more in line with the belief.

Those are the two choices: change the belief or change the behaviour. That is what this journey is about. It is about looking closely at the beliefs that you hold and asking yourself why you hold them. It is about observing the way in which you behave and considering if your actions fall out of alignment with your beliefs. It is about being present when you speak and identifying whether or not you speak from a place of authentic truth.

The experiences that I have shared could be anyone's story. I have learned along the way that as human beings, we have all had our share of hardships (or life lessons as I see them now). When you make the conscious decision to step into your own truth, to live with FIERCE Integrity, you are opening yourself to the possibility of a personal transformation, of transcendence. This process has the power to radically alter your life, but only if you are willing to let go and surrender. Are you ready to let go of your past? Are you ready to be accountable to yourself and others? Are you ready to surrender blame of any kind?

I would be lying if I said that this process, this FIERCE Integrity course, was easy. It isn't. It is hard work, and it requires dedication and commitment. Simply put, you will get out what you put in. Along the way, remember that learning to live from a place of authentic truth is actually more of a journey than a one-time lesson. You will fall. You will forget. You will blame and judge. The important part is to remember the truth so that you can get back to living from this place as fast as possible. When you live from this place of Integrity, of truth, of authenticity, you will be at peace. You will not suffer. You will be whole. The truth of the matter is that you already ARE all of these things...you have only forgotten.

~ Maren doing yoga on the beach in Chile, 2007

~ *Clockwise from top left:*
Maren ice climbing in the Nordegg area, 2006;
Maren and Trent on the summit of a mountain in the BC Rockies, 2007;
Maren, Trent and Chephren in the Okanagan, 2009

MAREN HASSE

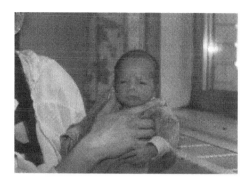

~ Clockwise from top left:
Ben as a premature baby, 1987;
Ben learning to use a cane, 1990; Maren and Chephren, 2009;
Erik and Ben, 2010

~ Maren and Trent in Chile, 2007

~ Brent Young, Photo Courtesy of Edwina Podemski

MAREN HASSE

PART II
FIERCE *Integrity*
A COURSE IN LIVING YOUR TRUTH

INTENTION-SETTING

Before we get into the course, I would like to share some insight on the importance of intention-setting. It is possible that you are already familiar and well-versed with the practice of setting intentions, but if you aren't, here are some things to keep in mind:

- Everyone is going to have a different way of setting their intentions. Some people do them verbally—for example, waking up each morning and choosing 1-5 intentions for the day and saying them aloud or to oneself. Some people write them down—in a notebook or on a computer. As for me, I have a "Divine Miracles and Healing" document on my computer which contains all of my intentions for all areas of my life: my health, my career, my family, etc. I check in with these intentions regularly and adjust them as needed.

- Intentions are a great tool for getting really clear about what it is that you want to create in your life. I actually use the term "co-create" as I believe that I am working hand-in-hand with The Divine in order to create my desired reality. (I will often use words like "Source," "God," or "The Universe" interchangeably to talk about the Divine. Know that it is not necessary to have this same belief in order for intention-setting to work for you.)

- Before you set your intentions, connect to your heart-centre. Sit quietly for a few moments and connect with your deep sense of inner knowing. Set your intentions from that place.

- From my experience, intention-setting can be one of the most powerful practices that you will ever engage in, but only if you believe in its power. If you don't believe in it, or only believe in it half-heartedly, it certainly won't have the same impact in your life.

- Once you have set your intentions, walk away. What I mean by this is put the pen down or close the document on your computer and acknowledge in your heart, mind, and soul that all has happened just as you intended it. Invoke a deep sense of knowing that all will unfold as you have intended it to, and live from this place.

If you are still not sure about how to get started, let's use this project as an example. Here are some examples of intentions that you could set for this course:

It is my intention that:

- This project assists me in stepping into my own FIERCE Integrity.

- This project serves and benefits me on my path towards living my highest potential.

- I commit myself fully to this project and will spend 10 minutes per day working on the exercises and reflecting on the process (notice the personal accountability/action step built into this one).

- As I step into my own FIERCE Integrity, it will improve my relationships with friends and family.

- If it resonates with me, I will share this project with others so that they too can receive the gift of this process.

Hopefully these examples will help to shed light on your own intentions for this course and assist you in aligning with your place of truth.

THE PAST

As you may have noticed, the first part of this book deals mainly with the past. Generally, I am not a big fan of living in or dwelling on the past, but I have found that, for the purposes of stepping into my own FIERCE Integrity, journeying into my past has been a valid, important part of my process.

While it is true that our capacity to create our desired reality lies entirely in the present moment, the past can help us by providing us with clues about what we need to change in order to create the reality we want. Human beings are often creatures of habit; in other words, they continually engage in repeating patterns of thought, word, and deed. We must shine light on these habits in order to change them.

In this part of the course, I am going to extend an invitation for you to look into your past. Before you do so, I need to be absolutely clear about something: it is of high value to walk into your past if you do so from your heart-centre. In other words, endeavor to leave the ego-mind out of it!

This is actually a lot more difficult than it sounds. As I wrote earlier, I wasn't entirely ready to share this story until recently because I was still hanging on to elements and feelings of being the "victim" of some of my past circumstances. When you open the door to your past, it can be easy to become overwhelmed with all of the "skeletons" that you encounter there. This is where intention-setting can be of real value to you.

Imagine that your past is a dark closet with a door on it. All of the experiences that you have ever had until now lie behind that door. When you journey into the closet, imagine that you are holding a flashlight and shining light on the memories and experiences that lie within that space. Some of those experiences are going to be painful to see again, scary even (those are the skeletons), and some will be light-filled and glowing of their own accord. Before you enter the closet, you can set your intention to only see the "skeletons" that you are ready to deal with. Your intention could sound something like, "I ask to see only what I am ready to see and that I may do so from my heart's centre. Please fill me with Divine Light as I make this journey and help me to see into my past from a place of my Highest Truth."

Part of what makes this journey into the past so difficult is that we must be accountable for all of our past behaviors. As I have related to you in the details of my story, I needed to get very honest with myself about the choices that I have made in the past. I had to gather up my skeletons and bring them out of the closet and into the light. What's more, once I brought them out into the light, I needed to see them as perfect, and acknowledge that those experiences and the emotions that they created were exactly what they needed to be.

Keep in mind that this whole process of stepping into your Integrity is a journey. In other words, you aren't going to be transformed overnight. If you are truly ready to step into your truth and be completely honest with yourself, know that it is going to require you to do some work—you must be FIERCE remember? If your deep sense of knowing is telling you to move forward on this path, then you are ready. Trust this sense of readiness.

Now, with this thought in mind (using the past as a place to look for clues instead of a place to find excuses), I would like to invite you to reflect on some of your perceived "skeletons."

Hint: if you still aren't sure what I mean by your skeletons, think about experiences that have caused you to feel regret, guilt, or shame.

Here are some questions to get you started:

Since the word Integrity often conjures up the notion of telling the truth (Integrity of Word), the first set of questions pertains to lying:

- Have you told some really big lies? Have you told some less-big lies? What are they?

- How about some "harmless" lies (often called white lies)— what would be some examples of those?

- Is there a pattern to the lies that you tell? In other words, do you lie consistently about the same thing(s)? To the same people? In similar circumstances?

The key here is to not go into the story of why you "needed" to tell the lie or why you now perceive that you told it. Don't make excuses for the lies, or even analyze them, just be willing to be accountable to yourself for telling them.

The next set of questions deals with emotions; specifically, emotions that we have deemed negative. Negative emotions can be very helpful as they allow us to see the parts of ourselves that need healing. They help us to identify the thought patterns that are causing us to have the most amount of suffering.

- Have you made choices that you now perceive as mistakes?

- Have you made decisions that have led you to feel regret?

- What are you ashamed of?

- Do you hold contempt, judgment, or resentment towards others? Who?

Again, the goal here isn't to feel sorry for yourself, or to wish things were different. Remember that each and every one of these experiences is a part of you. It is what led you to be exactly where you stand today. And you are EXACTLY where you need to be.

With that being said, if you are anything like me, this whole remembering process can be intimidating. I don't know about you, but I have told a lot of lies in my life. I have also made a tremendous number of mistakes. I have engaged in behaviors that I am not proud of. I have taken unnecessary and foolish risks. I have treated myself and others poorly. When I did this exercise for myself, all of my skeletons came piling out of the closet at once, into the blaring light of day. Having all of my "dark" thoughts, memories, and experiences come forward at the same time was overwhelming for me. It was like watching my past play like a movie in my head. It was an ugly thing to re-live and I ended up feeling terrible.

I am sharing my own experience of this exercise with you because I know that it doesn't have to be like that. It isn't necessary to look at it all at once, and in such a harsh way. As I said earlier, you can use the power of your intent in order to look at smaller, more manageable parts of your past. The key to it all lies in your ability to look at it from your heart-centre, from the place inside of you where there exists a never-ending well of unconditional love. When you unconditionally love someone, it inherently means that you forgive them.

So, BEFORE YOU ALLOW THAT TRAIN WRECK OF A MOVIE TO PLAY OUT IN YOUR HEAD, I need you to know where we are going with this. We are aiming for shining light on those lies (that is the remembering the past part) and then IMMEDIATELY moving into letting go of the lies, mistakes, and regrets, and forgiving yourself for making them. You heard me, I said let them go and then FORGIVE yourself. And no, I don't care what the lies were, how many mistakes you made, or how many people you hurt.

The truth of the matter is, you ARE NOT the lies that you have told. The "real you" is a perfect being, a DIVINE, loving soul. (To tell yourself anything different than this truth is the real lie, but we'll get to that.) For now, centre yourself in your heart. Hold a space of love and compassion for yourself and let the movie reel play.

THE PRESENT

We live in the present moment. An obvious statement, sure, but have you spent some time fully considering this notion?

From my perspective, the present is an exciting place to be! It is where all of the magic happens. I recently saw a picture circulating on the Internet expressing the importance of the present moment. It was an image of a digital wristwatch—but instead of a time being displayed the screen simply said NOW. What time is it? NOW! Think about that. Every time you ask that question, the answer is NOW. The time is now, the moment is now, all we really have is now. So, what are you waiting for? The present moment is all we know for sure. This type of thinking makes me appreciate how important it is to stay present.

Time is an interesting concept. As humans we tend to flit away the present moment by bending time. Oh yes! We are all masterful time-bending beings! How do we bend time? By dragging the past into the present and wishing the present moment away by sending our consciousness on into the future.

Thinking now about your own thought patterns, is it possible for you to identify which one of these dimensions you spend the most time thinking about? Do you find that you spend more time holding onto the past or more time projecting into the future? Remember, we aren't looking to judge ourselves for this type of thinking, we are simply hoping to bring some awareness to our thoughts.

When we hold on to the past, it is usually for one of two reasons. The first of these is that you are remembering the past in order to re-live happy memories of times gone by. This could be done by looking at old photographs, telling stories, or simply watching the memories on the screen in your mind's eye. This type of behavior is healthy and can bring about a lot of joy! These are the memories that are already light-filled in your closet of the past. Know then, that you don't necessarily need to change this type of behavior; simply bring your awareness to it. Merely being conscious of the fact that thinking about your past is bringing you out of the present moment is a huge step. In other words, if this behavior is serving you, don't change it, just be aware of it so that you can make the decision to do so on a more conscious level.

The second reason we go digging into our past isn't as light-hearted or healthy. We have already talked about the skeletons in the closet. When we dwell on these skeletons, we are clouding up the present moment by attaching ourselves to these memories and the emotions that they invoke within us. Every time we engage in this kind of time-bending behavior, we are robbing ourselves of what is happening in the present moment. Still not sure why that is a problem? Maybe an example will help.

Imagine that you are sitting by a stream. It is a beautiful September day. The leaves have just started to explode into their beautiful array of fall colors, and it is a few hours before dusk. You can feel the warm sun on your face as you close your eyes and inhale the sweet smells all around you. You can hear the trickling of the creek and then BAM! You are ripped out of the peace and serenity that is offered to you by your present surroundings. Instead, you are transported (time-bending, remember) back in time to an event that has caused you to feel deep resentment towards someone and shame at the way you handled the situation. You start thinking about everything that went wrong, and all of the things that should have been different.

Do you see my point? We so often fail to recognize the beauty that lies in the present moment because we are living in the past. The example that I gave is perhaps a bit extreme in that it was such an idyllic setting, but I would argue that you can find true beauty in each moment. Our senses are masterful at delivering external stimuli—sights, sounds, smells, sensations, tastes. It is up to us to be present and receive the gifts that are incoming all day long.

Similarly, when you project your thoughts into the future, you are again missing out on what is happening in the now. One reason that some people engage in this kind of thinking is because they believe themselves to be unhappy. This kind of thinking often sounds like "won't it be better when" or "I would be so much happier if." The sad thing is that this type of thinking tends to be a pattern; in other words, it repeats itself. How often have you longed for something—a party, a holiday, the end of university, a new job, retirement—and when it arrives, you are disappointed. Perhaps it wasn't exactly the experience that you'd hoped for, or perhaps it didn't go exactly as you'd planned. If that is the case, you are left with feelings of disappointment and unhappiness, with no way of reconciling them. Feeling disappointed and unhappy is not a comfortable state of existence, thus people again shift their focus into the future, hoping that what they are looking forward to next will finally make them happy.

Yet another way that we can project into the future is by worrying about it. Anxiety has an insidious way of creeping into the present. The funny thing is so much of what we tend to worry about as humans is totally out of our control! Our worries are often wrapped up in our insecurities (what will they think of me?) or our fears (what if something bad happens?).

If you are someone who suffers from anxiety, you are not alone. Anxiety disorder is actually the most prevalent mental illness in America right now, affecting between 10-15% of the population! The question is, what can you do about it? Well, I believe this course is a great place to start. This course will help you get in touch with the present moment. It will help you get at the truth of the situation and let go of the story in your head.

When we engage in these time-bending behaviors, we miss what is happening right now. Right in front of us. We miss the sound of our baby's giggles, we miss the warm, comforting feeling of the cup of tea in our hand, and we miss the beauty of the flowers blooming in our backyard.

It doesn't get any better than this. This moment. This now. This is it. You get to decide how to experience it, how to live it, and how you feel within it. So right now, get really present. Connect with your body. Go inside. Connect with breath. Connect with sensation. Centre yourself. Get connected with your inner "truth." In other words, find the place inside of you where the real you resides. Your most authentic self. The you that lies underneath all of the labels that the world has placed on you, and that you have placed on yourself.

Now, from that place, ask yourself:

- Do you feel that you live with FIERCE Integrity?
- If not, what is in the way of stepping into your Integrity?
- Do you tend to live in the past or the future? Be specific (and honest!) about which types of time-bending behaviors that you tend to engage in.

ACTION:

- Throughout the day, as many times as you can remember to, connect with the present moment. Simply STOP what you are doing and begin to bring your awareness into your body (feel into it, observe what is happening inside) and to your surroundings (use all of your senses, take it all in).

TO EXPERIENCE YOUR OWN
HEART-CENTERING MEDITATION
GUIDED BY MAREN HASSE,
VISIT WWW.FIERCEINTEGRITYBOOK.COM

INTEGRITY OF THOUGHT

The first part of this course deals with the Integrity of our Thoughts. When people think about living with Integrity, they will often think about the honesty of their words, reflecting about how often they tell the truth. They will also associate Integrity with how often their actions match up with their words. Said another way: Do they do what they say they are going to do? While our words and our actions do indeed reflect our Integrity, they originate from somewhere. It is our thoughts that actually create our reality, and determine our level of Integrity. It is our ability to be authentic and honest with ourselves that determines our ability to be honest with others.

It has been said that our conscious thoughts (that is, those that we are aware of) make up only between 2-10% of our total thoughts. In other words, between 90-98% of our thought processes are actually unconscious, or happening outside of our awareness! When I first heard this statistic, I have to say, I was shocked! How could I be completely unaware of so much of what I think?!

It makes sense when you think about it. Our senses are capable of taking in so many stimuli at once. We are constantly being bombarded by sights, sounds, smells, sensations. Can you imagine if our brains weren't programmed to discern what is necessary amongst all of this input? We would be completely overwhelmed!

In addition to taking in and processing stimuli, our brains are making unconscious judgments, assessments, and decisions based on the connections that exist within our neural networks. In other words, our unconscious mind is simply following the patterns that already exist within our brain. What creates those patterns in our brain is where it gets interesting. It is our conscious thoughts that create these patterns and associations in our brain; therefore, what we pay attention to creates our reality.

If you are still not sure what I mean, perhaps an analogy will help. Imagine that your conscious mind is the CEO of a large multi-national corporation. Given the breadth and the scope of the corporation, it would be absolutely impossible for the CEO to make every single decision that would affect the company. What the CEO can do is set policies and procedures so that the rest of his/her employees know what his/her wishes or intentions are for the company. Your unconscious mind represents everyone else that works for the company. It is simply following the orders and wishes of the CEO.

Throughout this course, we will be referring to the mind collectively as the ego or the "voice in your head." Calling it a "voice" is appropriate because it is your conscious thoughts, the thoughts you are aware of, the ones that you can "hear" inside of you. Note that the voice in your head is quite different than the inner knowing that you have, your intuition. This inner knowing comes from deep inside of you, from your heart-centre. This is worth mentioning here because sometimes what you know to be true in your heart doesn't match up with the voice in your head. It is actually these inconsistencies, between our heart and our head, which threaten our Integrity.

LESSON 1:

The Voice in Your Head

Our thoughts reside in our mind. Our thoughts make up the "voice in our head." Our thoughts are the voice of our ego.

It is important to qualify something here. Our ego isn't a "bad" thing. Sure, it may have a "bad" reputation, but only because it has the capacity to be misused. The ego has a valuable role to play in our journey towards profound transformation. It is what keeps us motivated and moving forward on our path. It contains the forces that keep us driving forward: the fear of failure, mixed with a desire to succeed. It is that voice of reason that ensures our basic physical needs are continually being met: our need for safety, for privacy, for security, for nourishment.

When you develop the ability to listen, truly listen, to the voice in your head, you can then begin to discern the information that you receive. In hearing that voice more clearly, more consciously, you will be able to glean more information about how that voice is affecting your current reality and therefore you will develop the ability to change that reality. In identifying the voice in your mind, you will begin to feel the difference between your thoughts and your instincts.

A while back, a friend turned me on to Julia Cameron's *The Artist's Way*. *The Artist's Way* is a fantastic book for assisting you in stepping into your creativity, and I found one of the techniques in the book really useful for getting at the voice in my head. The author calls this technique "morning pages." Essentially, you wake up each day and, before you do anything else, you sit down with a journal and engage in stream-of-thought writing. Stream-of-thought writing is exactly what it sounds like—writing every single thought that comes to mind. Even if you aren't sure what to write and nothing comes forward, you write THAT down, and then see where that thought takes you. (If it helps, I call this exercise "puking on paper"—colourful, I know, but for me, it helps me to step into the true essence of the activity.)

Here are some important things to keep in mind when doing this kind of writing:

- Try not to censor yourself. Allow yourself to write down everything that comes to mind. (If you are worried about someone reading your thoughts, keep your journal or pages in a safe place.)

- Don't go back and re-read or edit the pages. Allow them to stand alone after they are finished. We will be re-visiting them later on in the course.

- Don't worry about sentence structure, punctuation, or readability!

- Set a time limit for each writing session. 5 minutes is a good place to start. If you have more time, you can go for longer, but use a timer to keep yourself in check.

- Writing first thing in the day is recommended because nothing has really happened in your day yet—it is kind of like working on a blank canvas.

I would suggest trying to set some time aside for this type of writing every day for the period of time that you committed to this course. You will need at least a few days' worth of stream-of-thought writing in order to move onto the next lesson, so plan accordingly. If, however, you don't have time for this strategy, or it doesn't resonate with you, simply continue to sit in meditation and notice which thoughts fly across the screen of your mind.

Also, if you are finding the process of getting in touch with your inner voice difficult, or if you are surprised by what you are uncovering, don't worry! This is quite normal. The important thing is to stick with it. I recently had a coaching conversation with a woman who told me that until we started working together, she had never even entertained the notion that one could change one's thoughts! What I am trying to say is: start where you are at, and know that it is exactly where you should be on the journey.

QUESTIONS FOR REFLECTION:

- How in touch are you with the voice in your head?
- What is the quality of the voice in your head? Is it a kind, loving voice, or is it a judgmental one?
- Would you say that you have Integrity of thought?

ACTION:

- Begin to get in touch with the "voice in your head" by sitting quietly for 5-10 minutes every day. Remember to allow whatever arises to simply do so.
- Engage in stream-of-thought writing every day for at least one week.

Notes Lesson 1

MAREN HASSE

LESSON 2:

I AM Statements

In this lesson we are going to begin looking at the stream-of-thought writing that you began working on in the previous lesson. We know by now that often we are telling ourselves things that we aren't even truly aware of.

A while back, I attended a Byron Katie workshop (this woman is a Master Teacher of getting at that voice in your head). This workshop involved some stream-of-thought writing in which I was asked to get very child-like and write down any judgments that I had made within the past day, few days, or week. I was surprised to see/read/say aloud some of the statements that I had been telling myself.

One of these statements was (are you ready for this?): "I am gross." Gross. Who says that to themselves? Well, it turns out that I was telling myself that very cruel statement way up there in my head. I would never dream of saying that statement to anyone else, and yet, here I was telling it to myself. It was a huge eye-opener.

I have been studying Dr. Wayne Dyer's latest work about "I am" statements. In his book *Wishes Fulfilled*, he writes that the name of God as said to Moses in the Bible, is "I Am That I Am." In other words, when you say, I am… (whatever it is), you are essentially calling forth the Divine presence that is within you and manifesting it into existence. When you say "I am SICK," for example, your physical plane experience is going to show this reality to you, again and again, confirming the statement that you yourself have made. It has to do so in order to keep your ego-mind in alignment with reality. When your ego and reality fall out of alignment with each other, you are left in a state of cognitive dissonance, a state that is extremely uncomfortable for the mind. The mind is so uncomfortable in this state that it will do anything to get out of it, (even going so far as to physically manifest conditions that you don't want) in order to come back to a place of homeostasis.

ACTION:

- Scan the stream-of-thought entries and look for "I statements." Anything that begins with I... "I feel, I want, I wish, I am..." Highlight or circle them. (Different colored highlighters work well because we are going to be pulling out another category in a future lesson).

- Read all of the "I statements" aloud.

QUESTIONS FOR REFLECTION:

- Are you surprised by any of your "I statements"?

- Are you better able to hear the overall quality of your inner voice? Is it kind and loving, or cruel and judgmental?

- Which "I statements" would you like to change?

Notes Lesson 2

MAREN HASSE

MAREN HASSE

LESSON 3:

The Sliding Scale Technique

In the last lesson, we talked about the importance of those "I am" statements, and how they have the power to create your reality. Once you have identified which of these statements you would like to change, the first thing you need to do is look for evidence in your physical life that they aren't true. In my "I am gross" example, I said to myself, "If I was truly gross, it is unlikely that I would have a husband who loves me and wants to be intimate with me, or have friends that want to give me a hug when they see me." Then, you need to replace that "old statement" with a new one. A kinder, gentler one. For me, I found that it wasn't sincere to go from "I am gross" to "I am beautiful." What I am saying is that this new statement lacked Integrity for me, and therefore wasn't true. Much like when we set our intentions—if you don't believe the new statement you are trying to tell yourself, you are wasting your time.

Instead of going to the complete opposite statement, I decided that I needed to make the statement slightly truer. I call this the Sliding Scale Technique, which calls for making slight changes to the statement you are trying to change, aligning yourself with the new statement, and then making yet another incremental change. I have found that this technique works well because it is easier to align your beliefs with small changes rather than large ones.

In the "gross" example. I said to myself, "I am not that gross." Looking at the evidence to support this new statement, I could genuinely believe it to be true—and therefore this statement had Integrity for me. Once I believed that "I wasn't that gross," I was able to say, "I am not gross at all," and that quickly became, actually, "I am really quite cute." During this time, I also spent a great deal of time looking at myself in the mirror and telling myself these nicer things. Louise Hay calls this "mirror work" and it truly does work!

To give you a sense of just how powerful this tool is, consider this. I discovered this "I am gross" statement in my head in October of 2011, and spent the month of November 2011 in Maui on vacation with my family. Throughout my holiday, I spent a great deal of time walking around in a bikini and telling myself increasingly kinder things using the Sliding Scale Technique. In that 6-week time period I LOST 10 POUNDS WITHOUT CHANGING A SINGLE THING EXCEPT THE VOICE IN MY HEAD!!! You see, my physical plane reality had no choice but to call into existence that which I truly came to believe!

I share this story with you because I know that so many of us struggle with body image issues. I have struggled with them my whole life! Whether we believe that we are too fat, too skinny, too ugly, too old, or too freckly, we can be masterful at telling ourselves that we are anything less than perfect, just as we are. So before you jump onto the next fad diet bandwagon, consider instead looking at the belief system that has likely led to a lot of your insecurities in the first place.

Once you start to love and appreciate your body for exactly what it is, you will start to feel better inside and out. Remember that your reality has no choice but to align with your beliefs. Part of this journey also involves time. In order to change our beliefs about ourselves, we need to let go of our need to time-bend into the future (I will be prettier when I lose 10 pounds) or the past (I looked so much better when I was younger).

When you start to love yourself and your body as is, you will automatically start to change your behaviours as well. You will take better care of yourself. We tend to take care of the things that we love and cherish and abuse the things that we don't. We will address some of these behaviors (our habits, our eating) when we talk about the Integrity of our Actions.

ACTION:

- Looking at the "I Am" statements that you have made, choose one that you would really like to change.

QUESTIONS FOR REFLECTION:

- How does this statement make you feel?
- Are you certain that it is true?
- Can you find any evidence that it isn't true?
- How do you think you would feel if you were able to change this statement to one that was more loving?
- Can you think of a statement that is more in alignment with what your heart knows to be true? Can you make it more loving?
- Can you accept this more loving statement as true and let go of the old story in your mind?

ACTION:

- Rinse and repeat! Do this same exercise with as many of your "I Am" statements as you'd like!
- Continue to work on each of these statements using the Sliding Scale Technique.
- Be patient with yourself! Your physical reality will absolutely change as your thoughts do, but it can take some time for your outside world to catch up with your inside world. Focus your attention on looking for evidence that things are indeed shifting!

Notes Lesson 3

Lesson 4:

Our Judgments of Others

In today's lesson, I want to invite you to go back to your free-writing pages and highlight or underline those statements that sound judgmental, especially those that sound judgmental towards others. These include comments like: "She should..." or "If only he would..." or "How could she..." You can also look for judgments of situations, which might sound like "If only that wouldn't have happened", or "It is too bad that..."

Next we are going to talk about our assumptions. According to the dictionary, the word assume means:

1. To take upon oneself: assume responsibility; assume another's debts.
2. To undertake the duties of (an office): assumed the presidency.
3. To take on; adopt: "The god assumes a human form" (John Ruskin).
4. To put on; don: The queen assumed a velvet robe.
5. To affect the appearance or possession of; feign.
6. To take for granted; suppose: assumed that prices would rise.

7. To take over without justification; seize: assume control.

The meaning of assume that we are dealing with here is #6—when we make assumptions about another person (e.g., they should do this), we are "supposing" about their actions. We are essentially buying into a story in our minds that is telling us that we know what is best for that person. From my perspective, how could we possibly know what is best for another person when we have no idea what their true reality is? Just imagine for one moment what the voice in their head might be telling them.

One thing that I have come to realize is that when one human being is acting in a way that seems cruel, ignorant, hateful, or arrogant, they are being at least as critical or hurtful towards themselves on the inside.

We have all been there. We have all been mistreated. We have all been "victims" of someone else's cruel actions or hurtful words. The key word here is victim. When we adopt a victim mentality, we become completely at the mercy of another person's actions or words. We entirely give our power over to them essentially saying, "Ok, here you go, make me feel as bad as you wish."

When I say it like that, it sounds ridiculous, doesn't it? The point is, we cannot control the actions or words of another person, we can only control the way that we react to their actions or words. In essence, we have a choice.

Perhaps another example will help. A few months ago, someone said some very, very hurtful things about me to my husband. My husband, for whatever reason, chose to share these words with me. My initial reaction (yes, I reacted), was to feel shattered! I was devastated by the hurtful words and went straight into the shower to cry. I allowed myself to feel the pain of the words, to release all that it had triggered inside of me.

But then, it happened. I remembered who I really am. I remembered that these emotions I was feeling were simply a message from deep within me, showing me my insecurities about myself that I hadn't totally healed. I became grateful for the message and the opportunity to release some of this pain I was holding on to, and instead of feeling resentment towards the person who had said those things about me, I felt gratitude. After all, his words wouldn't have hurt me if some part of me didn't believe in them myself. Furthermore, I know that it is only when someone is in pain themselves that they lash out towards others, which allowed me to turn my anger towards that person into compassion. I took a few deep breaths and allowed myself to be filled with Grace. For myself and for the other person.

You are not going to stop being hurt. There are going to be times when you are mistreated. The choice that you have is to see these experiences as gifts, as messages from your soul. It is the light shining on the dark parts that lie within you, that lie within all of us. You have a choice of blaming the other person and remaining a victim, or releasing them from that blame and being accountable for what is truly yours. Remember that we are the creators of our own reality, and it is up to you if you want to stay in a state of suffering.

QUESTIONS FOR REFLECTION:

- If you find yourself making assumptions about another person, first ask yourself, is that your role? Is it your duty to assume or suppose about what is best for another person? Do you have all of the information in order to make these kinds of sweeping generalizations or preconceptions about other people?

- Think of a time when you allowed someone to hurt you. Are you willing to release that person from blame? Are you ready to own those emotions as yours? Are you ready to forgive?

Note: When you change the way you feel about a person or a situation, it doesn't necessarily have to "look" any different on the outside. For instance, you might forgive your brother for all of the wrongs that you have perceived he has done to you, and yet, you might not wind up being the best of friends. Once you have done the work of forgiveness, you also release any expectations of what that relationship will be. In other words, you hold that person in a state of Grace or unconditional love, which means that you feel that way about them regardless of how they choose (or don't choose) to love you back. Remember, you can't control another person's actions or emotions, you can only choose your own.

Notes Lesson 4

MAREN HASSE

LESSON 5:

Button-Pushing

In the last lesson, we talked about releasing our judgments of others. We talked about how when someone says something that is hurtful towards you and you react, you are in fact only reacting to something that is actually within you. This same work can be applied to situations and experiences in our everyday world.

Have you ever heard the expression, "That really pushes my buttons?" I use this statement a lot. It means that something has happened that really annoys you or disturbs your peace. It could be something like the actions of another person (the work that we did in Lesson 4), or it could simply be a situation that you find frustrating: a flat tire, a long line up, spilling coffee down your shirt, etc.

When something pushes your buttons, it is again an opportunity to see something that lies within you. In other words, it isn't the situation that is disturbing your peace, but a story in your mind associated with the situation that is really your problem. You are judging the situation, assuming that it needs to be different than it is, and we all know where judgments lead us! They drag us back into that victim mentality, where everything is happening to you and the situation lies out of your control.

I want to talk briefly about the word control. The truth is, we don't control anything. We like to think that we do, we like to plan and organize our lives, but the truth is that control is truly an illusion. We can't control circumstances—but what we can control is our reaction to them. We get to choose whether to be accountable to ourselves or to be a victim. When we choose to be accountable to ourselves and own up to our reactions, it can help you to release that which is no longer serving you and exist in a state of peace.

Let's look at an example. My number one "button-pusher" is my son Chephren. He seems to have a gift for lining up experience after experience that simply drive me crazy. Before I became a mother, I would have said that I was a "control-freak." People around me confirmed this image of myself by using words like "A-type personality" and "perfectionist." When I became pregnant, I had a plan. I was going to have a "perfect" pregnancy and a natural childbirth, I was going to breastfeed, and everything about my journey into motherhood was going to be just...perfect. The thing is, looking back on it, my experience was perfect, although it ended up being totally different than what I had planned! Quite literally, every expectation that I had going into motherhood was unmet. You know from reading my story that initially, this perceived loss of control sent me into a depression. This too was perfect. It was a strong message from my soul that something was very wrong with my belief system. In order to regain my sense of peace and wellbeing, I had to learn to let go of my expectations and instead live very much in the present moment.

Recently I was visiting with friends, people that I haven't known for that long whom I met through my yoga practice. During this conversation, a few of them shared with me that they perceived me to be an easy-going and light-hearted individual. Easy-going? Light-hearted? Me? I couldn't believe what I was hearing. When I got home later that night, I sat in reflection and I saw the truth of their statements. When I looked deep down within myself, I saw that I had changed. Letting go of the old story that told me I needed to be in control had allowed something new to come into my being. Or to look at it another way, you might say that I was more in touch with my true essence than I had been previously.

It is important to clarify something here. My "perfectionist" quality isn't bad, it simply isn't serving me in the same way anymore. There are wonderful advantages to this facet of my personality: great organizational skills, efficient time management, punctuality, and producing results. I would say that I still have access to these valuable skills. The difference now is that these skills no longer define me.

Each time my son (or any other person or situation) manages to push my buttons and disturb my peace, I immediately try to determine the story that is associated with my reaction. What is the voice in my head telling me about what is happening here? I have talked about some of these stories earlier in the book. My inability to breastfeed had the story "I am not a good mother" tied to it. Similarly, my need for a C-section had the story "I am not a real woman" tied to it. Both of these stories were very harsh "I Am" statements that I needed to heal. Chephren's existence, exactly as he was and is, provided me with the opportunity that I needed to bring these belief systems, these stories, into my conscious awareness.

Button-pushing situations don't have to be as dramatic as this. Another one of the situations that Chephren has created for me (and continues to create) is his ability to throw a tantrum. Now, cognitively, I know that most children throw tantrums. I know this, and yet, each time he throws a tantrum, especially if there is someone else there to witness it, I react. First I am flooded with emotions: frustration, anger even, and then shame. All wonderful triggers and messages from my soul. What story are they associated with? Again, the same old story about "I am not a good mother." Each time I feel these emotions, it presents me with yet another opportunity to let go of this story and bring that part of me to back to a state of wholeness.

My son has been one of my greatest teachers. He continues to push my buttons every day, leaving a mess almost everywhere he goes, climbing higher than I would like, having tantrums in the most public of places. I can't control him—and now that I think about it, I wouldn't want to. My job is to guide him and teach him. To treat him with the utmost respect. When he chooses to engage in acts that push my buttons I can immediately choose to receive the gift and forgive both myself and him, returning us both to a state of Grace.

QUESTIONS FOR REFLECTION:

- What types of situations really push your buttons? Can you identify the story in your head that is associated with them?

- Is there someone in your life who really pushes your buttons? Can you see them as bringing forth the wonderful opportunity for healing? Are you willing to forgive them? Are you willing to return both of you to a state of Grace?

TO HEAR FURTHER TEACHINGS THAT CORRESPOND WITH LESSONS 4 AND 5, VISIT WWW.FIERCEINTEGRITYBOOK.COM

MAREN HASSE

NOTES LESSON 5

MAREN HASSE

Lesson 6:

Finding the Divine Perfection in EVERYTHING!

So far in this course, we have been talking about first identifying the voice in our head, and then letting go of the judgments that we hold both towards ourselves and others. We have been working towards letting go of our assumptions and changing the story in our head. We have been working on letting go of blame and becoming accountable for ourselves and our emotions.

Now, I would like to take it one step further. I want to invite you to do something wild! Something crazy! I would like you to think about each of those people or situations that you have made judgments about. Can you see each of these people or circumstances as Divinely perfect?

Remember that when you find yourself holding on to negative thoughts and emotions, the only person that you are hurting is yourself. You are the one that is causing the suffering in your life. You are the one who is allowing your inner peace to be disturbed. I am well aware that what I am asking you to do is no easy task. In fact, you could call it our life's work. However, while it might be a lot of work to change our perspectives about ourselves and others, it is well worth the effort. For as we develop and cultivate unconditional love and compassion for all sentient beings (including ourselves), it can pave the way to a more peaceful existence. This simple truth has the ability to alleviate a lot of your suffering.

One of the greatest minds of our time, Albert Einstein, said "In the middle of difficulty lies opportunity." What an invitation to find the Divine Perfection in each moment, especially during those times of struggle. Every single time I find myself out of my centre, back in a state of turmoil and inner suffering, I employ the mantra "Everything is perfect." It is what it is. One of the behaviors that I used to engage in was the need to know why events were unfolding as they were. "Why are Ben and Erik sick?" "Why is Chephren throwing yet another tantrum?" "Why is my marriage falling apart?" "Why is that person being mean to me?"

The truth is, you don't get to know why. It just is. In order to bring yourself back to center, you need to surrender this need to know. You need to simply allow. You are not in control, remember?

QUESTIONS FOR REFLECTION:

- Looking at your own circumstances, are you willing to let go of judgment entirely and see the people and/or situations in your life as perfect?

- Are you willing to surrender your need to know why things are as they are?

Notes Lesson 6

MAREN HASSE

MAREN HASSE

LESSON 7:

The Attitude of Gratitude & Receiving the Gift

I am a big fan of gratitude. I take the time regularly to sit quietly with my journal and actually write down all of the things I am thankful for. I even have a special journal that I use only for this purpose.

In May 2012, I had the privilege and pleasure of hearing Louise Hay and Cheryl Richardson speak at the I CAN DO IT Conference in Vancouver, BC, and was inspired to take my gratitude practice even further by cultivating a sense of gratitude on more of a daily basis. Waking up each morning and thanking my bed for wrapping me up and holding me through an amazing, refreshing sleep, thanking my closet for holding all of my beautiful clothes/accessories, thanking my shower for its ability to make me feel refreshed, clean, renewed. This daily practice has profoundly changed my life for the better, and I encourage you to try to bring more gratitude into your life on a consistent basis.

I recently had a coaching session with a client and we talked about how to avoid feeling disappointed when something doesn't go the way you'd hoped or expected. I am sure that most people can relate to this feeling on some level; after all, since when has absolutely everything in the world gone "according to plan"? I would argue though: wouldn't life be totally and utterly boring if it did?

For example, have you ever had the experience of being "pleasantly surprised"? Or how about wanting something to happen, having it not happen, and then looked back six months from then and said "Oh thank goodness that didn't happen!" Sometimes something that we perceive as "bad" might actually have the power to bring something "good" into your life. The point that I am trying to make is that while we are indeed creative beings who possess the ability to manifest our reality and make choices in our lives, there is also something bigger than us at work.

When we release our expectations (and quit time-bending into the future), we make ourselves more present and able to receive the gifts that lie in the now. We quit thinking about the way that we think things "should be" and allow them to be what they are, and what they are is perfect. The truth is that in each moment, you are exactly where you need to be. When we surrender to this truth, we find our centre. We find ease. We find the peace that lies within.

QUESTIONS FOR REFLECTION:

- What are you thankful for?
- What gifts are you willing to receive today?
- Can you think of something that you had once perceived as "bad" and look back and see the gift(s) that lie within that experience?

ACTION:

- Keep a gratitude journal. Write down as regularly as you'd like all of the things that you feel grateful for. I often do mine on a full moon, and call them my "Full Moon Gratitudes." Choose a regularly scheduled time that works for you.

- Sign up for the Receiving Project. It is an amazing and free e-course, facilitated by Jo Anna Rothman, an intuitive coach. This project will jumpstart your natural ability to receive gifts from the Universe.

Notes Lesson 7

INTEGRITY OF WORD

For a course that you may have assumed was mostly about "not lying," notice that it has taken us up to Lesson 8 to get at the Integrity of our speech! As you have now seen, living with FIERCE Integrity involves so much more than the words we say (although those are important too).

If you would like to cultivate more honesty in your speech, the first thing that you need to do is get really present while you are speaking. We have talked at length about the detrimental impact that time-bending behaviours can have on us; however, when we speak, it is especially important to be here now.

When you are truly present with your speech, and you are speaking from the place of your truth, it is much easier to hear the lies that you are telling, both to yourself and to others. To this day, I still catch myself saying things that are less-than-true. When this used to happen to me, I would just continue talking, telling myself that it didn't really matter. But it does matter. Each time you catch yourself telling a lie, and you choose not to do anything about it, it chips away at your Integrity. Imagine your Integrity of Speech has a form; let's use the analogy of the form of an egg. Each time you tell a lie, and you become aware of it but choose to let it go, you make a small chip into that egg. Eventually, after you have told enough lies, and chipped away at the egg, it will eventually break, changing forms completely. In other words, you lose sight of who you really are.

In today's society, lying is a rampant human behaviour. I recently heard that the average person tells three lies every ten minutes when they are having a conversation with someone else! To be honest, I have no idea whether or not this is a true statistic or not, but when I look at my own behaviour in the past, I can see how and why it might be at least somewhat accurate.

So why do we lie? Well, the reasons are many. As you can guess, it has a lot to do with the voice in our head and the stories that we are telling ourselves. It also has to do with making assumptions about others. Sometimes we lie out of habit. We say things or relay information that we have never even thought to question. We simply perpetuate the myths that we have accepted as true. There are even times when we lie to protect someone, or to help them hold onto happiness and hope for just a while longer—the lie of Santa Claus, for example.

Perhaps at this point, you are thinking that I might be leading you down a path towards "radical honesty." There have been a lot of funny movies made about this topic, including "Liar, Liar" with Jim Carrey and "The Invention of Lying" with Ricky Gervais. In both of these movies, one of the characters has been rendered incapable of telling a lie, obviously for entertainment purposes, leading to all manner of hilarious situations. While I can appreciate the humor of these types of movies, that is not what I am after. What I am aiming for is for you to have Integrity of Speech—and yes, there is a difference between this and radical honesty.

LESSON 8:

At Baseline - Evaluating the Accuracy and Integrity of Your Speech

I have already admitted (repeatedly) that I have told lies in my past, many of them! When I did the work around the Integrity of my own speech, I was shocked at how many lies I found myself telling. Once I decided that I wanted to commit to changing this behaviour, it was a matter of first being really present with my speech. At first, it was pretty awkward. In the past, I have tended towards "speaking before thinking," which means that I really needed to slow things down when I talked. Because of this tendency, I would often catch myself telling the lie, and then say, "No, wait. That's not entirely true..." and then change my words to be more accurate. Over time, I have found that I tend to pause and think before I speak—not always, but increasingly. In that pause, I try to remember to connect with my heart-centre, the place of my Divine truth, and speak from that place. I try to leave my ego out of it! It doesn't always happen like this, but it's a process, and one that I am enjoying growing into.

When you are engaging in observing the Integrity of your own speech, be gentle with yourself. Know that this type of awareness isn't going to happen overnight. It is going to take some patience and it will come with practice. When you start to discover the types of lies you tend to tell and the reasons why you tell them, first and foremost, be willing to forgive yourself! Remember that you deserve to be held in a state of Grace!

Questions for reflection:

- On a scale of 1-10, how accurate/honest would you say that you are when you speak? (10 = you never ever lie, think radical honesty; 1 = you lie to just about everyone, all of the time).

- Thinking about the lies that you have recently told, or have told in the past, can you start to see any patterns? Do you tell the same types of lies? (See below for a description of various types of lies).

- Are there situations in which you seem to consistently lie (meeting new people, being with people who push your buttons)?

- Are there certain people you consistently lie to?

Action:

- Begin to bring an increased awareness to your speech. Challenge yourself to speak with 100% accuracy.

Types of lies:

1. Lies that overstate or exaggerate.
   These types of lies are common when we really want to make a point or spice up the story. They can also pop up when we aren't totally sure of the exact story, so we embellish a bit.

2. Lies that understate.
   These types of lies are used when you don't want to let on that things are as bad as they are.

3. Lies of omission.
   Pretty self-explanatory. You deliberately leave out entire parts of a story in order to deceive or to save face.

4. Half-truths.

   We use these when we don't want to own up to the whole story, only part of it.

5. Complete fabrications.

   These are the big ones. Lies that involve no elements of truth whatsoever.

Notes Lesson 8

LESSON 9:

The Lies We Tell

We have been looking at the Integrity of our speech, looking for patterns in the lies that we have told in the past and continue to tell. Once we have started to establish some of these patterns, they can be very illuminating in helping us identify the story in our head about the situation we are lying about.

While it would be difficult to provide an exhaustive list of all of the reasons why we lie, there are some general categories that emerged when I did my own work in this area. Here they are, in no particular order:

1. Lying to protect someone

It is my belief that, generally speaking, human beings are quite kind-hearted and loving by nature. Actually, some people are so kind and gentle that they engage in lying behaviours repeatedly. In these types of lies, the person telling the lie is doing so in the hopes of protecting someone's feelings. When you lie to protect someone, your intention is to do no harm. This is a valid intention, but not a valid practice, because it helps to affirm to yourself the story in your head that you "are a liar" and therefore you "don't have Integrity." Even with a positive intention, it still has the ability to chip away at the egg.

I would like you to consider the fact that when you lie with the intention of protecting someone you are basing this lie on assumptions that you have made. For example, a few months ago, a friend of mine opened a yoga studio and asked me to teach at her studio. I said that I would be interested in doing so (and at the time I was). Later in the process I found out that the studio is one that teaches the same "routine" each time, and this is something that does not appeal to me as a yoga teacher. While I knew that this did not resonate with me as a yoga teacher, I also didn't want to let my friend down. The time came for me to arrive at her training and I did not really want to go but felt that I should. I thought about calling her and making up some excuse for not going, but this would certainly not be living my Integrity! My husband thankfully, pulled me out of the "story in my head" and said, "Why don't you just tell her the truth?" Ah, yes, the truth. Why didn't I just tell her the truth?! So, that is exactly what I did, and the response that I got was, "Thank you so much for your honesty!" You see, I had assumed that I would let her down or hurt her feelings, but the reality is that she wanted instructors working for her who could share in her vision! By giving up "my" spot, it made room for someone better suited to her studio to come in, and freed up my time to be available for classes that worked for me.

Another example is when someone asks you your opinion about something. You know the questions: "Do I look good in this?" "What do you think about this new recipe?" "How does the couch look there?"...etc. We get asked questions like this very often, and each time it has the potential to threaten our Integrity, especially if we have a less-than-kind opinion of whatever they are asking us about. So what to do? Go back to your intention of "doing no harm." Can you be honest but in a kind way? Is there a gentle way of conveying your true feelings? On a related note, sometimes we can be forthcoming with our opinions even though we weren't asked for them. For this type of situation I would remind you of the old adage, "If you don't have anything nice to say, don't say anything at all." Remember, there is a difference between speaking with Integrity and radical honesty!

2. Lying because of feelings of insecurity or inadequacy

I know this type of lie well because it is the type of lie that I have told the very most in my own life. One of the stories in my head has to do with the belief that "I am not enough." Not good enough, not fast enough, not smart enough, not pretty enough...you get the picture. When I allow myself to be governed by these stories of inadequacy, I find myself lying to save face. For me, these feelings of "not enough" result in a perceived need to exaggerate or embellish my stories. If I buy into the story that my story isn't good enough or exciting enough, then I find myself making it a better story, adding details that aren't entirely accurate in order to "spice things up."

I engage in a similar behavior when I am not quite sure of something. My ego tends to feel humiliated if I don't know the answer to something, and I have found myself on more than one occasion responding to questions even when I am not sure about the accuracy of my statement. As both a teacher and parent, I believe that my child and students will respect me so much more if I say, "You know, I'm not sure, let me get back to you on that one," or, even better, "I'm not sure, why don't we Google that?" (I am so grateful to live in a time where "Google" is a verb!) Not only will this help to cultivate their respect for me, but it will affirm to them that I respect them.

3. Lying because we have never taken the time to consider what we are saying

Sometimes we lie without really even intending to. This can happen easily when we aren't totally present with our speech, we aren't even aware, or have never taken the time to consider the accuracy of our statements. So much of what we believe is based on information that we have taken on unconsciously. We all hold in our minds beliefs that we have simply adopted as truths, without questioning their validity. There are many examples.

One that comes to mind is the belief that having an only child is "irresponsible." Without knowing it, I used to hold the belief that only children are at risk for developing social problems, and therefore, I needed to have more than one child. I continued to experience guilt, shame, and fear, especially each time someone asked me when we were planning on having our second child (button-pushers!).

The problem was, my head and my heart couldn't agree, and I was in a state of cognitive dissonance. I knew in my heart that I didn't need to have another child, especially not from a place of guilt or fear, but my head continued to perpetuate this very fear-based story. One day, it occurred to me that I needed to look deeper into this story. I got onto my computer and did a few hours' of research on the topic. The conclusion that I came to was that only children are in fact, statistically no more likely to develop social problems than a child with siblings. Interesting. Just like that, my fear-based story evaporated, and peace about the topic was restored!

The problem with these types of lies is that they can be hard to detect. One way that I have gotten around this problem is to recruit the help of my family, specifically, my husband. Trent has a knack for "calling me out" on inaccuracies of my speech. It is one of his gifts and it used to push my buttons. Now, I am more able to receive the gift of his need for accuracy and in fact, we have turned it into a little game. We call it "Mythbusters." When one of us (it goes both ways now) makes a statement that isn't entirely accurate, we call out "Mythbusters!" and go running to the nearest computer to Google whatever statement we are calling into question. Instead of feeling inadequate, humiliated, or ashamed, I find that I am grateful for the opportunity to refine my speech and my beliefs to an even greater state of Integrity.

Now, I am very aware that one shouldn't believe all of what one reads on the Internet. It is the process that is important here. It's the willingness to call into awareness old beliefs that you are holding onto and embracing the opportunity to let them go.

4. Lying because I am trying to deceive myself or another

As a society, I would argue that these types of lies are ones that we are less tolerant about. These tend to be the lies that we find harder to forgive, things like cheating, stealing, and outright lying about what happened, where you were, who you were with. These are the types of lies that, when told, carry a great deal of shame and guilt. And when these feelings of shame and guilt come bubbling up, we tend to layer them with yet another set of lies, until we completely lose sight of the truth of who we are. These lies are dangerous. Not only do they have the ability to hurt others, but they present the greatest threat to our Integrity.

MAREN HASSE

If you have told lies of this nature in the past, then the first step is to let them go. Forgive yourself. Move on. You need to make a conscious choice to leave them in the past. These types of lies are some of the skeletons that lie in our closet. Earlier in the course, we talked about the need to address some of these skeletons. Remember that we are not dragging them into the light to re-live them in a painful way. We are not doing this to perpetuate our feelings of blame or judgment towards ourselves or others. We are doing this to shine light on the dark. To love even these "dark" parts of ourselves and to release our feelings of blame and judgment. We are standing in the here and now and being accountable for our actions.

Perhaps you will feel like you need to make amends for some of these past behaviors, perhaps not. How you come to a place of releasing yourself from these negative feelings and return to holding yourself in a state of Grace is up to you. Check in with your heart. It knows exactly what you need to do. Remember, there is no part of you that isn't worth loving.

Notes Lesson 9

LESSON 10:

Who Do You Lie To?

Think about all of the people in your life. Are there people that you lie to more than others? Once you have identified these people, go back and ask yourself the question from our previous lesson: "Why are you lying to them?" (Remember to think about any assumptions that you might have made).

I realize that this process can seem a bit overwhelming or intimidating at first, so I want to offer an example from my own life in order to help frame this exercise for you. In my world, the single person that I lie to the most is my child. When I ask myself the question, "Why do I lie to him?" here is what comes forward:

1. Give an example of a lie that you have told and identify why you think you told it:

•   Sometimes I lie to my son when I feel as though I am "losing control" of the situation… if you are a parent, you know what this looks like. In the past, I have been totally guilty of threatening to take away things that I couldn't or wouldn't (e.g., taking away all of his books), or in my frustration, making huge sweeping statements that didn't make any sense ("I am never taking you shopping again!").

2. Next, identify the assumption that you have made:

- Assumption: This lie will serve to "control" the behavior of my child.

3. Finally, identify the truth or reality of the situation:

- Reality: This child knows that I can't or won't follow through, and the behaviour continues/escalates!

Once I have identified this lying pattern, I can now begin to work hard at changing it. Instead of making grandiose statements, I focus on making promises that I can/intend to keep. This has been a great change for both of us. Because I am able to be more consistent with the consequences that I set, Chephren is much more likely to change his behaviour if he knows that I can (and I WILL) do what I say I will do.

Here is another example, using this same process:

1. The lying behavior:

- In the past, I have often lied to "protect" my child. These are often lies of exaggeration, where I tend to overemphasize the potential consequences of his actions. For instance, "Wash your hands or you are going to get sick!"

2. The assumption:

- If I tell him all of the "bad things" that could happen, he will stop the behaviour.

3. The truth:

- This has the potential to create a fear-based worldview in my child!

When I started to look at this set of lies, I realized that instead of creating some fear-mongering fabrication for the situation at hand, there was always the opportunity to use more gentle, loving language to explain it. Using this new strategy, my example, "Wash your hands or you are going to get sick!" became, "There are germs on your hands, and we need to wash them off before we eat." Same result, totally different message. Another example that fits under this category is "Be Careful! You're going to fall!" Instead, this becomes, "Be aware of where you are putting your feet! I am here if you need me." It gives a totally different message.

Questions for reflection:

- Thinking about all of the people in your life, who do you tend to lie to the most?

- What kinds of lies do you typically tell them?

Action:

- Once you have identified your patterns of lying behavior, see if you can identify any assumptions that you might be making. Connect with your heart-centre. Is your assumption correct? Is there any chance that there might be a deeper truth that you are overlooking?

Notes Lesson 10

LESSON 11:

Are There Any Good Lies?

There is a category of lies that we have yet to address. These are the "good" lies, the ones that we tend to justify. These types of lies include lies that indulge in the land of fantasy and all of the magical characters and creatures that lie therein. This category of lies also includes things like light-hearted gags, and fun experiences like magic shows or surprise parties.

So far in this course, I have asked you to become very present, bringing as much conscious awareness as you can onto your thoughts and your words. Along the way, have you come across lies that you have told with full, conscious awareness? Lies that you have told yourself were entirely justified? When I was learning to step into my own FIERCE Integrity, I came across lies such as these. The Easter Bunny...Santa Claus... I absolutely did not have the heart to tell my young son that they were merely fantasy! I told myself that the "spirit" of these characters was real, and therefore, it was a lie that I could justify telling. At the same time, I was having difficulty integrating this behaviour with my commitment to living with 100% Integrity. Was there a grey area? Could there be one?

Another example that came forward was the fact that I love practical jokes. I grew up in a house where my stepdad was constantly playing them on his friends, and we had a lot of laughs over them. These experiences make great stories, stories that are fun to tell and re-tell again and again. I have played a few of these types of jokes myself over the years, and when I looked into my past, I was unsure of whether or not this kind of behaviour was chipping away at my Integrity.

Similar to how I feel about the concept of "radical honesty," I decided that I didn't need to adopt such an extreme viewpoint of the world to have FIERCE Integrity. What I needed to do was come up with a set of guidelines that would help me to determine if the lie I was telling or the behaviour I was engaging in was in fact threatening my Integrity.

Here are the questions that I now ask myself before I consciously tell a lie:

- What is my intention? Is it to do no harm?
- How would I feel if this "trick" were played on me, or if this lie was told to me? Also, think about the people involved—will they appreciate the humor of the situation? Are they the type of people who can laugh at themselves?
- Will the truth eventually be revealed? In other words, how long will the lie be prolonged?

I feel like these reflective questions were really able to help me integrate practical jokes and surprise parties into my Integrity; however, I was still wavering about the childhood mythical characters. When it comes to engaging in imaginary play with my son, no problem! I love imaginary play and believe that it is essential to childhood development. I will play "house," school" or "going on an airplane" all day long with my son, but when it comes to Santa Claus and the Easter Bunny, I still felt out of alignment with my Integrity.

So, I needed to go deeper. When I break it down, I have come to the conclusion that it isn't the actual make-believe characters that bug me, but all of the other "stuff" that tends to come with them. At Christmas, Santa seems to have become a symbol for excessive consumption. At Easter, the Easter Bunny symbolizes a huge amount of low-quality chocolate and treats. The mere existence of these situations in our current culture has always pushed my buttons, but once I had my son I was in a position where I felt like

I had to perpetuate it! Thankfully, I was able to reflect on the fact that if something pushes my buttons, it is an opportunity to look within myself. Essentially, it reminded me that this is my issue, not my son's.

This awareness led me to see that this issue is hugely tied to my actions. If I was going to justify these lies, and not allow them to chip away at my Integrity, it meant that I needed to make sure that my actions strongly corresponded with my true values. For example, I needed to demonstrate that while Christmas was indeed about the magic of Santa Claus, it was also a time to feel gratitude, appreciation, kindness, and love for one another. I needed to make these holidays less about the treats and presents, and more about quality time with the people that we love.

In my story, I shared with you one of the strategies that I used in order to deal with this dilemma in my life. If I wanted my son to grow up valuing people instead of things, I needed to change my own behaviour, thus MareBare Necessities was born—my year of non-consumption and "living with less." In other words, my Integrity moved into the world of Action.

QUESTIONS FOR REFLECTION:

- Do you tell lies that you feel totally justified in telling? What are they?

- Are there lies that you are less sure about? Can you find the story attached to these lies and shed some light on your uncertainty?

Notes Lesson 11

INTEGRITY OF ACTION

You have probably heard the expression, "Your actions speak louder than words." I really believe in this statement. At the end of the last lesson, we were talking about how I wanted to try to teach my son the real meaning of special holidays like Christmas. I knew what I wanted to be different (spend less time and money on gifts and more energy on being together), but talking about this desire wasn't enough. I needed to live it.

Lesson 12:

A Look at Your Habits and Daily Routine

We are going to start this part of the course by looking at our habits. When we talk about habits, we are referring to the stuff that you do consistently, whether it be daily, weekly, or monthly. Analyzing our habits and routines, we can gain a lot of insight into whether or not we are living our Integrity.

Perhaps some of our habits run in direct opposition to what we hold as truth in our hearts. An example of this would be regularly engaging in a behaviour that you feel ashamed about. This could be anything, but some examples could be: gossiping, drinking, smoking, or watching trashy shows on television. In your heart, you know that this behaviour isn't in line with your values, and yet, you find that you are engaging in it anyway.

On the other hand, perhaps our intentions aren't reflected by our actions. A good example of this is having a monthly gym membership that you underuse or, worse, don't use at all. I myself have engaged in this type of behaviour, and my local gym was my "charity of choice" for a while! In this kind of example, your intentions are good, but you haven't been able to follow through.

Questions for Reflection:

- What is your daily routine? Run through it, start to finish, in your mind. Make a list of your activities. What do you do every single day? Every week? Every month?

- Looking at your list, would you say that you are a person of habits and routines? Are you attached to those routines? How much of your "routine" were/are you not even consciously aware of? What are the things that you just "do" and don't give much thought to? Are there "good" habits on your list? How about "bad" habits? Notice how you feel when you think about those habits that you perceive as good/bad.

In doing this exercise myself, I have come to a few conclusions. The first of these is that by creating an attachment to habits and routines, I may be limiting the possibility of creating something new in my life. For example, in driving the same route each day, or by always ordering the same thing at the same restaurant, or by taking my son to the same park over and over, I realized that the Universe has to work even harder to bring something new into my life! If you are someone who feels "stuck" (and I know that a lot of people have felt that way at one time or another) simply switching up your routine(s) can have a drastic effect on the way you begin to show up in the world. You can "unstick" yourself simply by stepping aside and allowing the new to flow in!

The second thing is, if you have a routine and/or a good/bad habit and it is working for you, fine. BUT, the key is to know WHY you are engaging in that behavior. For example, one of my evening routines is to sit down with my husband and watch some "mindless" television. We actually don't have cable, but we do have access to Netflix and other shows on iTunes via our Apple TV. For a long time I was beating myself up about this "bad behaviour"... telling myself that I "should" be doing things that are more "productive." Worse, I often would couple this "nonproductive" behavior with a glass of wine. (Can you hear all of the self-judgment here? The story in my head is quite insistent that TV watching and wine drinking are "less than acceptable" behaviors—especially when they are combined!) You can see how this simple habit that I have been engaging in could interfere with my ability to feel that I was living with FIERCE Integrity. And we do this type of thing all of the time don't we? We eat the chocolate, we drink the drink, we miss a workout and we use these behaviours against ourselves to say, "See? See? You don't have any Integrity! You can't change the way that you are!"

So, how do we deal with this type of situation? Well, you really have only two choices—you can stop the behaviour altogether (which is really tricky—especially if it is a long-standing habit) OR we can begin to look at the reason behind it. In other words, we can change the voice in our head.

For instance, in my TV example, it looks like this:

Okay Maren, WHY are you engaging in this behavior? What purpose is it serving? To which I answered (honestly and with Integrity): Firstly, it is something that my husband and I can enjoy together (this is important because if my primary reason for the behaviour is spending time with Trent, then we can look at other things that we might like to do together instead). The other reason is that at the end of the day, I am just "done." I am tired, I am (often) stressed, and I just want to engage in something that doesn't require me to think (also important to know).

Now that I've done this "work" and brought some awareness to the situation, I automatically begin to have more compassion for myself. The voice in my head becomes kinder and less judgmental. I can see that my motivations for the behaviour are valid (at least they are to me) and I can therefore be kinder to myself whenever I choose to engage in them. I also begin to feel empowered to change the behaviour by looking for ways to fill those needs in a different way. For example, Trent and I both enjoy playing the guitar and this has replaced some of our TV sessions. Do we still watch TV on occasion? Absolutely. But I am finding that it is happening less now than it was before and when it does happen, it doesn't feel as "bad." In other words, my habits are more in line with my Integrity.

QUESTIONS FOR REFLECTION:

- Can you apply this strategy to some of your own habits and routines?

- What actions are you engaging in that are preventing you from feeling like you are living your Integrity?

- Can you identify the story in your head and change it to one that is more loving?
- Can you replace those behaviours with different ones that offer you the same effect?

Notes Lesson 12

LESSON 13:

Does Your Work Reflect Your Integrity?

This next lesson is about your job, or what you do for a living. This area of our lives is well worth exploring, especially given the fact that we spend as much time at work as we do! As I write this, it occurs to me that in today's society, this category might not be as straightforward as it sounds. For some people, this category really is about their job, while for others, it might fit under other names such as "student" or "stay-at-home parent." Some folks might be retired, or self-employed. Others may be unemployed or be committed to volunteering at various organizations. It doesn't matter which of these categories you fit into. What matters is what you are telling yourself about your current situation. (Yes, more about that voice in your head!).

Whichever category you find yourself in, here are some questions for reflection:

- Are you happy with your current situation? Why or why not?

- Is what you do (the job you have, the degree you're taking, or organization you volunteer for) in line with your belief system? Why or why not?

- If you could wave a magic wand, what would your perfect "career" look like? If you are no longer working, then ask yourself, "How would I like to spend the bulk of my time?"

- Is there a disparity between your current reality and your ideal reality? If so, what do you perceive to be in the way between **WHAT YOU WANT TO DO AND WHAT YOU ARE DOING?**

If when you answered these questions, you identified that you are perfectly happy in your chosen career or occupation, and that it aligns perfectly with your belief system and ideals, then that is wonderful! Your job will most certainly reflect your Integrity and you can move on to the next lesson. If, on the other hand, you find that your career does not resonate with your belief system, or if you find that there is some disparity between what you do and what you want to do, then read on.

Let's begin by looking at the answer to the last question: "What do you perceive to be in the way between what you want to do and what you are doing?" It is my belief that people will often stay in a job that they hate because of fear. Fear in this category manifests itself in all kinds of ways: fear of failure, fear of the financial "risks" of changing careers, and fear of being vulnerable and "putting oneself out there." If fear is one of the barriers that you are facing, what are you afraid of? Identifying your fear will help you to uncover the story behind it.

Next, notice if your ego (the voice in your head) is making you out to be a victim. In other words, if your reason for staying in a miserable career sounds like, "My family/partner needs me to because...." or "If only my partner would..." then you are living a victim mentality. In other words, you need to own the fact that you are choosing to do what you are doing. No one else. You.

Unless you are willing to let go of this victim mentality and own up to the fact that you are the only one who can change your career path, then it will be very difficult to create the change that you desire. If you continue to focus on all of the reasons why not, you will continue to bury all of the "wouldn't it be great ifs." Recognize the fact that choosing to do a job that is out of alignment with your values is a choice. You and only you are responsible for your situation.

Now, before you up and quit your job, I want to be clear about something. I am not suggesting that you do anything of the sort!

I am simply asking you to bring some awareness to the work you do, why you are doing it, and what are you telling yourself about it. Perhaps with this awareness, you will change your career, perhaps not. Before you do anything rash, beware of the "Grass is Greener Syndrome." This is a nasty affliction in which the person in question makes a decision with very little awareness in the hopes that something better will come along. Quite often, when we make decisions in this way, we end up in a situation that is worse than the one we fled from!

Remember in Lesson 6 when we talked about Divine Perfection? This is another opportunity in which to employ this mentality. Can you find the Divine Perfection in your current situation? Can you find ways to confirm that you are exactly where you need to be? Can you identify any gifts that you might be missing or have previously been unable/unwilling to receive?

If your job is a source of suffering for you, you essentially have two choices: change the way you think/feel about it, or change your job. That's it. Which path you choose is up to you, but I would encourage you to grab your flashlight and shine the light of your awareness on what is truly going on here. If you are being held by fear, can you let that fear go? If you are living with a victim mentality, can you change the story in your head?

It is possible that by simply being accountable to yourself, and owning the fact that you "do what you do," you might feel better about it. However, if, after spending some time exploring the story in your head, you decide to make a change, simply know why you are doing it. Allow yourself to be guided by your heart as you begin to live in a world of possibilities.

Notes Lesson 13

LESSON 14:

What's on Your Plate?

This lesson is all about the relationship you have with your food. At first, it might sound strange to think of us having a relationship with our food; if this is a new way of thinking for you, bear with me, it is relevant. In this lesson, you are going to be reflecting deeply about the foods that you typically purchase, prepare, and consume. You are also going to be considering how or why this bodily necessity could take us out of our Integrity.

To begin with, ask yourself the question: How do I feel about food? Most people will answer this question with, "Great! I love food!" and I would have to agree. Food is indeed wonderful! But while this initial reaction to food is valid, I would argue that it is also superficial. In Western culture, there is more to our relationship with food than meets the eye. For instance, more people than ever before are struggling with food-related maladies, whether it be heart disease, diabetes, or obesity. I am interested in this area of study, and also in the fact that we as a society are so quick to point fingers of blame away from ourselves as consumers. So many of us are playing the role of "victim" to the food industry. Hopefully by now you will have started to see that being a victim is only a story in our minds—and the good news is that means that it can be re-written!

Our food relationship consists of purchasing our food, preparing our food, and eating our food. Each one of these categories has an impact on our Integrity.

QUESTIONS FOR REFLECTION:
Purchasing your food:

- What kinds of food do you mostly eat? Are they packaged foods, convenience foods, restaurant meals, homemade meals? Foods of many different colors, textures, and variety? Foods from different ethnic backgrounds and origins? Locally-sourced food? Organic food?
- Where do you usually purchase your food?

Preparing your food:

- Do you cook?
- Do you like cooking?
- Who do you cook for?

Eating

- Who do you typically eat with? Where do you typically eat?
- In an average day, how much food do you eat?
- Do you snack throughout the day or consume a few big meals?
- Do you have "rules" that you follow with respect to your diet? Did you set these rules or did someone else (like your doctor or your spouse)? How do you feel about these rules? Do you follow them?
- What types of emotions are tied to your eating behaviours? Specifically, do you feel any negative emotions such as: fear, guilt, shame, blame, judgment, or anxiety?

I realize that this is quite a large and potentially overwhelming set of questions; however, it seems to accurately reflect the complexity of our relationship with food. As you briefly scanned these questions and reflected upon them, did any "red flags" jump out for you? Can you readily identify any areas where your Integrity could be threatened?

If you are not sure what I mean, perhaps some examples from my own life will help. I would consider myself a fairly health-conscious individual. I am physically active, I teach and practice yoga, and I generally try to purchase, prepare and consume fresh, healthy, and organic foods for myself and my family. I generally love to cook and have chosen to follow a mainly vegetarian diet. When I look at the list of the above questions, it is readily apparent where I can easily "slip" and fall out of my Integrity. For me, behaviours like using a microwave, eating convenient or "junk" foods, eating non-organic foods, eating out, overeating, and eating on the run all have the potential to threaten my Integrity.

With respect to the last question ("What types of emotions are tied to your eating behaviours?") my answers have varied widely. As you know from my story at the beginning of this book, my own personal relationship with food has been complex. The binging-purging behavior that I had engaged in during my teens seemed to have somehow altered how my body was able to digest and process food. I suffered from severe bouts of anemia, requiring that I get injections of iron under my skin. I also suffered from intense episodes of intestinal pain, bloating, and discomfort for which my doctor could find no cause. As you can well imagine, when I ate, I tended to feel a great deal of fear and anxiety, as I wondered whether what I was eating was going to make me feel awful.

After subjecting myself to numerous tests, and after visiting several specialists, it was determined that I had IBS, or Irritable Bowel Syndrome. This is not a great diagnosis, due to the fact that nobody knows what causes it, nor if it can be effectively treated. I was quite unsatisfied with this result and decided to take matters into my own hands.

Throughout my twenties I tried many, many different diets. I tried a vegan diet for about six months, consuming no animal products. I tried several other lifestyle diets (Body for Life, the Blood Type Diet, and the South Beach Diet) to no avail. I still suffered from

IBS symptoms and, what was worse, no amount of exercise seemed to make a difference in the way I looked or felt, either. For most of my 20s I was about 20-40 pounds overweight and, to make matters worse, I was tired all of the time. Finally, after years of trial and error, I tried a celiac diet. Avoiding wheat products altogether seemed to offer me the most relief, and I started to have more energy and see improvements in the way that I looked and felt.

I followed a celiac diet for approximately three years, until I got pregnant. For some reason, eating wheat products during pregnancy didn't seem to affect me in the same way as it had before, and I gradually re-introduced them throughout my pregnancy. Flash forward through the pregnancy and the post-partum depression, and, as you might guess, I had little energy or will to obsess about the food that I was eating, especially during the first year.

My interest in food intensified again when I committed to my "living with less" project. During this project, I made a concerted effort to eat strictly within the confines of my belief system. I grew as much of my own food as possible, I prepared a lot of our food from scratch, I tried to source all of our food locally and if not local at least organic, and I even took a brief sojourn into the world of foraging! It was a wonderful learning experience, and I believe that as a family we benefited substantially from my efforts. Eating in this way made me feel great. I had more energy and, for the most part, my IBS symptoms seemed to have resolved.

I found that changing our lifestyle so dramatically required that I do quite a bit of research. Along the way, I discovered a whole host of other reasons to be afraid: namely carcinogens and other chemicals in our foods! Pesticides, BPA, GMOs...the media is full of information on all of the dangers that lurk in our supermarket. Again, I found myself eating with a lot of fear and anxiety, but now I was afraid for my whole family!

I would love to be able to say that after my year-long experiment was over that all of my healthy eating behaviours have remained, but they haven't. I found that some things simply took too much time and weren't practical or sustainable for me to continue. Since the end of my project, I have continued to focus my energy on trying to balance my values with what is realistic for me in terms of time. I have also attempted to find a balance between acceptable and unacceptable "risk" in terms of the dangers that are now inherent within our food system.

As you know by now, despite my very healthy lifestyle, I was still carrying around a bit of extra weight until recently. The final piece of the puzzle fell into place when I was able to change the voice in my head. It was through this realization about the power of the voice in my head that I was able to reach another fascinating conclusion: I realized that what I was telling myself while I was eating was as important, if not even more important, than what I was eating! In other words, how we feel about what we eat affects how our food is processed and digested by the body! Put simply, our emotions matter.

Can you think of times in your life where your eating behaviors have been tied to your emotions? If you aren't sure what I mean, here are some examples that might help:

- In my family, we often eat when we are happy—for example, when we're celebrating something special with an indulgent meal.

- Some people find that they eat when they are sad—for example, reaching for a bucket of ice cream and a single spoon.

- As was the case in my teens, some people use food to express self-loathing or to try to gain a sense of control. This can be played out in our pathologies around food, from obesity to anorexia and everything in between.

- More recently, I have been focusing on eating from a place of gratitude. As you will see, focusing on this emotion while you are eating can have tremendous benefits!

The point is, we are emotional beings and how we are feeling quite often affects the choices we make about our food. The reason that this is relevant is that when we eat without a lot of awareness or consciousness, we aren't connected with the "why" of our behaviour. And quite often, the small self or ego has all kinds of messages to tell us about what we "should" or "shouldn't" be eating. As with the exercises we did in the "habits" section, can you connect the dots for yourself here? Are there eating behaviours that you are engaging in that you perceive as "wrong" or "shameful"? Can you identify the beliefs that are leading you to these feelings?

It might be as simple as creating an intentional, mindful space when you purchase, prepare, or eat your food. As much as possible, I shop at farmers' markets and connect with the people who are growing my food. I get a weekly "Organic Box" delivered to my door full of fresh produce. I try to only buy meat and animal products from a local and ethical source. My vegetarianism is based on my own Integrity. I don't eat animals because I know that I wouldn't be able to kill an animal to eat it. I am not saying that these are things that you should do, but this is what I know to be true for me. I also know that when I am in situations where living in this way isn't as readily available to me (when I travel for instance) I can still forgive myself and change the voice in my head to one that is more gentle and less judgmental.

In my everyday life, I try to bring mindfulness into my interactions with food. For instance, when I am cooking, I try to make it more of a meditative experience by being as present as possible, taking in the colors, textures, and smells. I think about who I am preparing the food for. Often it is for my family and/or friends, and I connect with the energy of being of Service to them. There are many stories floating around about how cooking with love makes the food taste better and from my own experience, I can say that it's true!

Whenever I eat, as often as I can remember, I offer up some gratitude for the food I am about to eat and ask that it be put to my body's best use. You don't have to do this publicly; I often will do this silently in my head. I simply stop, bring myself to the present moment, and cultivate feelings of gratitude, connecting myself to the energies of the earth, sun, and all of the plants, people, and conditions that had to be present in order for me to receive this beautiful, nourishing gift. I attempt to savor my food, to truly enjoy it. As a result, I tend to feel satisfied with less food. From my experience, eating with mindfulness has profoundly changed my life!

I believe that as a result of simply changing my beliefs about food and the holding a space of gratitude and appreciation when I eat, I have affected the way my body is able to process and digest food. I am not a scientist, but from my own experience, I can tell you that letting go of fear and changing the story in my head has radically changed the way that I feel in my body.

I am very aware of the fact that the food relationship is going to be more complex for some people than others. Some people are fortunate to have never fallen out of alignment with their highest self when it comes to food. They inherently know what is best for their bodies to consume and they do so with reverence and gratitude. Or you may, like me, find that your relationship with food is complex and one in which you will have to work really hard to come into alignment with your Integrity.

ACTION:

- Purchase, prepare and enjoy a meal served with love and gratitude!

Notes Lesson 14

MAREN HASSE

Lesson 15:

Your Fantastic Five

This lesson is all about the people that you surround yourself with. I was in a yoga class one day and the teacher shared the following quote with us: "You are the average of the five people you spend the most time with." (E. James Rohn) At the time, I was lying in Shavasana, the pose that comes at the end of every yoga class in which you are simply lying still on your back, and when I heard these words, I felt them sink deep within me. After class, I continued to think about this quote as I began to integrate it into my current belief system.

Going back to Lessons 4 and 5, we talked about how our relationships with others can provide profound opportunities for self-reflection. In other words, what you see and react to outside of yourself is essentially a mirror for what is happening within you. When you think about the five people you spend the most time with, notice that these people are therefore your biggest mirrors, or your greatest teachers, depending on how you choose to look at it.

Back in Lesson 5, I shared with you some of my experience of parenting my son. I reflected that he is truly one of my greatest teachers and yes, he is indeed one of my "fantastic five." I have chosen to see him as truly fantastic, but it took some time to get there! Another one of my "fantastic five" is my husband. Trent and I are completely different, and yet, according to my theory, he is one of my biggest mirrors. It took me a long time to see this as true, and our marriage suffered greatly as a result.

At one time, the "story in my head" about Trent and about our marriage began something like, "We would be so much happier if only he would..." The ending to this sentence varied over the years: be nicer to me, like the same things that I do, be more spiritual, help out more around the house, etc., but the theme was the same. I believed that he needed to change in order for us to be happy as a couple. We fell into a holding pattern over the first 10 years of our relationship: we would get frustrated and want to end things, go traveling and make up, come home and get frustrated all over again. We would travel because we found that we seemed to always get along whenever we were away from our daily responsibilities.

This pattern only intensified after we had a child together and this time, there was no running away from our responsibilities! Our son needed both of us and ideally, he needed us happy, healthy, and not frustrated with one another! As you know from my story, we were far from living this idyllic reality (at least for the first few years of my son's life, anyway).

In April of 2011, things had gotten so bad that I was very seriously contemplating leaving my marriage. Given my own experience with dealing with the divorce in my family, it was far from the reality that I wanted for my son, but I seriously couldn't see any other way. A few weeks later, when Brent died, it felt like Trent and I were picked up and thrown back together, as if the Universe was saying to us, "You two are not done yet!" Even though we mourned for our friend very differently, we were bound by our common grief. Coming together with our community of close friends served as a reminder of everything we would stand to lose should we choose to go our separate ways.

During this time, when I was sharing with a friend how angry I was with Trent and giving her my best "If only he would..." lines, she simply said to me, "Trent is perfect for you. Exactly the way that he is. He doesn't need to change a thing." Well! My initial reaction was to hang up on her, but instead I bit my tongue and wrote down her words in my journal. After our call ended, I stared down at the words on the page and somehow, I knew that they were true. I was struck then by the profound realization that it was me that needed to change. If Trent was acting as a mirror for me, he was showing me all of the things inside of me that I didn't want to see.

It didn't happen overnight, but gradually, over the course of the next few months, our relationship came out of the dark and began to creep back into the light. I began to see old patterns within myself and began to look for new ways of doing things. For instance, I discovered a pattern where I would ask Trent a question, answer it for him, and then give him heck for giving me the wrong answer! Talk about making assumptions!

I started to ask him questions about things that were important to me and then I would just wait for an answer. Once I learned to wait and be still, and he began to see that he could indeed be honest without me attacking him, he began to come out with some brilliant insights that I am sure he has had all along—I had just never given him the space to share them.

Trent is a perfect mirror for me. He is my complement in almost every way. When I look at the Taoist symbol for yin/yang, it reflects what I now know to be true about our relationship. Much like the image in the symbol, we are two parts of the same whole. The best part is I am now learning that who we are in this model and how we relate to one another isn't permanent, it's ever-changing. Some days I am more "yin" and he is more "yang," and other days it is reversed.

I bring all of this forward now because I believe that there is tremendous value in looking into the biggest mirrors that you surround yourself with. Many of these mirrors will be family members, and even though you may or may not have chosen those relationships, they are perfect for showing you exactly what you need to see. It is up to you whether or not you want to look in the mirror and receive the gift of their reflection.

QUESTIONS FOR REFLECTION:

- "You are the average of the five people you spend the most time with." (E. James Rohn)

- Have you ever heard the above quote before? If so, what did you think of it, or did you even consider it? If not, take some time to think about it.

- Who are the five people that you spend the most time with?
- What do you think of these five people?
- Now think back to who you surrounded yourself with one year ago. Is it different?
- How about five years ago? Different again?
- Do you notice any changes or can you see patterns?
- What are the main attributes of the people that you spend the most time with?
- Do their values align with yours?
- Thinking back to your five people, what qualities do you most love and appreciate about each of them?
- What qualities do you find less-than-desirable?
- Do you think any of them "needs to change"?
- Are there people who you spend time with but don't really want to?
- If so, why do you?
- Do you feel that your "fantastic five" represent Integrity in your life?

NOTES LESSON 15

LESSON 16:

Your Hobbies

In this lesson we are going to draw awareness to your hobbies, or, in other words, how you choose to spend your free time. For the purposes of this lesson, let's define free time. Free time or spare time is any time that you have throughout your day when you are not bound by responsibilities or meeting your essential physical/bodily needs in some way.

When I sat down to write about this topic, the first thing that immediately came forward for me was the fact that there are two "camps" when it comes to free time: those who have a lot of free time and therefore have the potential to feel bored, and those who have far too little free time and therefore have the potential to feel stressed. In my life I know people from both camps, so I wanted to make sure that I covered all of the bases.

A LOT OF SPARE TIME

QUESTIONS FOR REFLECTION:

- How do you spend the majority of your time?

- Do you find that you are often bored?

- What activities do you do that make you feel as though you are "filling your cup"? (*See below if this is a new term to you).

- How often do you do these kinds of activities?
- What do you tell yourself about how you spend your time?
- Are there activities that you do often that you "wish you wouldn't"? What are they? Why do you continue to do them?
- Are there new hobbies that you are interested in learning but never have? Why not? What is in the way?
- Now, think of the activities that you do that you would consider "Being of Service" to yourself? What activities do you do in which you feel as though you are "Being of Service" to others?

Not a lot of spare time

Questions for reflection:

- How much "spare time" do you have on average each day?
- Can you think of ways that you might be able to create more time/space in your life to do the things that you want to do, instead of the things that you have to do?
- What activities/behaviours could you do less of? Which ones would you like to do more of or add in?
- Are you accessing help/support of those around you? If not, why not?
- Do you feel as though your cup is full? (*See below if this is a new term to you). What activities do you do to fill it? How could you build more of these activities into your daily life?
- Now, think of the activities that you do that you would consider "Being of Service" to yourself? What activities do you do in which you feel as though you are "Being of Service" to others?

*Filling Your Cup: If you haven't heard this expression before, it means activities that you do to feel good. When your "cup is full" it means that you would feel rested, renewed, and recharged.

ACTION:

- Make a list of activities that fill your cup. They can be short activities (playing a song on the guitar), medium activities (taking a bath) or long activities (going on a retreat). List as many things as possible, from simple to complex.

Regardless of which camp you find yourself in alignment with, whether you have too much spare time or not enough, how you spend the time that you do have matters.

In this lesson we have been talking about this notion of "filling your cup." We described these activities as things that you do to feel good, to feel rested and renewed. When I have done this activity with some of my clients, they had no trouble at all coming up with a long list of cup-filling activities. For others, simply coming up with a list was a challenge. But why is this important? Well, it is important for a few reasons.

The first of these is that when you take care of self, you can then have the energy to take care of others. You will be a better wife, son, employee, parent. You will be able to be more present when you are with the people that you love or doing the work that you care about. If you deplete your own resources by giving of yourself and you don't take the time to restore them, you won't be able to continue giving. Essentially, you will fall out of alignment with your Integrity, simply because you are too tired or depleted to do anything else! Taking care of self is to honor oneself, and honoring oneself is a component of living with FIERCE Integrity.

One of the difficult truths here is that sometimes honoring yourself can mean letting someone else down. Perhaps you have to cancel on a friend at the last minute or maybe you can't take on that overtime shift that your boss needs covered. The line between what you "should" and "shouldn't" do becomes very blurry as we try to navigate our way through making these everyday decisions. I am not suggesting that you blow off all of your obligations and commitments, but I am asking you to stop and connect with your inner truth as you move through these events. Above all, when you are making these decisions, remember to be kind to yourself. Let go of judgment and be willing to forgive yourself no matter what happens!

Cup-filling activities are important for another reason too: they simply feel good! I can be having a dreary or even dark day, and if I commit to 20 minutes of a cup-filling activity, afterwards the world looks different. For me, something that has always filled my soul is music. I have always enjoyed listening to music and I try to bring music into my life every day in some way, shape or form. Recently, back in February, I committed to learning to play the guitar. I had been trying to teach myself to play for about 10 years and I finally decided to simply commit to a daily 20 minute practice. At first, I was awful, but after about four weeks I slowly started to improve. After eight weeks, I could play a few songs and now, a few months later I can play and sing along to about forty songs! Am I going to win a Grammy? It is highly unlikely, but my heart and soul are full each time I pick up that guitar! Today, it is still one of my main "cup-fillers."

Another way to fill your cup can be to help others, or what I like to call "Being of Service." Most people have had the experience of how good it feels to help someone else. Many people are committed to volunteering with various charitable or non-profit organizations and find this work to be incredibly fulfilling and inspiring. While this type of work is wonderful, we can expand this notion of "Being of Service" even further and bring it into even more areas of our lives.

A simple way to bring yourself more into alignment with "Being of Service" is to change your intentions. Simply setting your intention around an activity to "be of the Highest Service" to all involved can change your experience of the activity drastically. I had this experience as a yoga teacher. At one time I would have to say that I was a "reluctant" yoga teacher. I liked the idea of teaching yoga but not the practice of it. When I looked deeper into this, I discovered that the "story in my head" about teaching yoga was that I felt like a "fraud." In other words, my ego wanted me to believe that I wasn't good enough to teach others. When I changed my intention about teaching yoga to one of Being of the Highest Service to every student I teach (and to myself), I started to enjoy it a lot more. I knew that if my intention was to be of Service then the rest would take care of itself, and it has.

Notes Lesson 16

MAREN HASSE

Lesson 17:

Clear the Clutter

I have talked throughout this book about my project of living with less. Not surprisingly, a year of minimizing my consumption also called into question all of the items that I had purchased or accumulated in the past, my belongings that I not-so-lovingly refer to as my "stuff." You know the "stuff" I am talking about: your furniture, your books, your clothes, your trinkets, your dishes, your appliances, your sporting equipment, your tools... the list goes on and on and on. These are all things that take up space in your life both physically and mentally.

You might be wondering, "What the heck does my 'stuff' have to do with my Integrity?" but the truth is, they are closely linked! Your belongings also hold a mirror for you with respect to the story in your head. Perhaps you have a lot of stuff and it results in a cluttered feeling in your home. A need to hang on to things could be tied to a story of lack in your mind, something like "You never know when I might need this," or "I am afraid that I won't have enough someday." Perhaps you own a whole bunch of stuff that you can't afford and owe a lot of money because of it. The story there might be something like "If I have all of this nice stuff, maybe I will attract the right people, the right job, the right circumstances into my life."

Whatever the case may be, your stuff says a lot about you. Your clothes are a great example of that, as they are literally a costume that you don every morning as you choose how you would like to show up in the world. Have you ever considered this before? If you haven't ever given this topic a lot of thought, here are some questions to help you go deeper.

QUESTIONS FOR REFLECTION:

- Would you say that your belongings represent your Integrity?

- How much stuff do you own? Is it more than you need? How much more than you need?

- Do a visual scan of your home...how do you feel surrounded by your belongings?

- Are there areas in your home that you feel better or worse about? What is it about those areas that makes you feel good or less than good?

- What kind of clothes do you wear or buy? How do you feel about your clothes? How do you feel about your closet? What does your wardrobe say about you?

ACTION:

- If you are dealing with too much stuff in your home, can you find 20 minutes per day that you could commit to reducing your clutter? If you have a family, can you get them on board to help you?

Not sure where to begin? One of the phrases that I used when I was going through all of my stuff was William Morris' quote: "Have nothing in your house that you do not know to be useful or believe to be beautiful." Also, I didn't try to tackle it all at once; I went through my house a little bit at a time. When I got stuck on items that I wasn't sure about, I took the time to get really present and decide from my heart-centre if this item was something that I needed to hang on to, and quite often, it wasn't. Another phrase that I used when I was going through my stuff was "Could someone else use this more than me?" The answer to this one was almost invariably yes, and I made a commitment to passing along as much of my still useable stuff as possible. This ties into the "Being of Service" idea we discussed in Lesson 16, and it felt really good to pass along my excess stuff to those organizations and people in need.

Notes Lesson 17

Lesson 18:

Buying New Stuff—Consumption

Now that we have spent some time thinking about all of the stuff that you currently own, I want to invite you to spend some time thinking about all of the "things" that you continue to acquire. After my year-long project, I feel as though I could write a book almost entirely on this topic alone, but for the purposes of this course it is my intention to simply bring some simple awareness to your spending habits and practices.

QUESTIONS FOR REFLECTION:

- What do you spend your money on?
- What motivates you to shop?
- Are you content with the amount of money that you spend and what you spend it on? If not, what would you like to change?
- Do you feel as though your spending reflects your Integrity?

After a year of non-consumption, you may or may not be surprised to hear that I have returned once again to the land of the consumer! However, while I do engage in the practice of buying new things, the way in which I go about it is quite different. One of the things that I try to do before I spend money on something (new or used) is pause. I pause, take a breath, get present, and ask myself if this is something that I really want and/or need. I ask myself questions that reflect my values/ideas about consumer goods: Is it well-made and will it last? Who is the producer and what are their company values? Is this something that I really, really love or am I just buying it because it is a "good deal"? How does it fit in with the other "stuff" that I have? If it is a home decor piece—where will it go? If it is a piece of clothing or jewelry—what do I already own that it can go with?

I have broken a lot of my own spending habits (buying things because they are on sale, buying things because I am bored or unhappy) by bringing some awareness into my shopping. Similar to the lesson on food, I am aware that this topic is something that I know some people struggle with a great deal and others not at all. As always, take what resonates with you from this course, and leave out what doesn't!

To hear more about Maren's views on "conscious consumption," visit www.FierceIntegrityBook.com

Notes Lesson 18

MAREN HASSE

Lesson 19:

Mental and Emotional Clutter

Are you a list-maker? A lot of people make lists, either on sheets of paper, notes on the phone, or mental lists. The interesting thing about lists is that, while they can be useful in helping us to get things done, paradoxically they can also serve as a reminder of all of the things that we haven't done yet. In other words, they have the ability to clutter up our consciousness and re-affirm the message that "we can't do it all." This is where lists can get us into trouble with living our FIERCE Integrity.

If you are a person who struggles with to-do lists here are a few tips that I have found to work well for me:

- It might sound obvious, but take action! Scan your lists and if there are things on that list that will take less than five minutes—do them!

- When you are feeling like you "will never get it all done," you won't! Instead, focus on telling yourself "I have all the time that I need to finish what needs to get done." You can also throw in affirmations about how efficient you are and how effortless it all seems.

- Pick the things on your list that you dislike the most and do them first!

- Delegate and/or ask for help. Sometimes we really do have too much on our plates. Know how to lean on the people around you when you need it most.

- At the end of the day, focus on all of the things that you DID get done and offer yourself up some genuine gratitude!

As a working-from-home mom, I often struggle with the anxieties that come with needing to get it all done. The above strategies work for me (when I choose to use them) and help me to live my Integrity.

NOTES LESSON 19

MAREN HASSE

WRAPPING UP

So far in this course we have taken a journey. We have taken the time to thoroughly explore our thoughts, our words, and our actions, as they each impact our ability to live with true, authentic, FIERCE Integrity.

By now, you might have discovered that this is not necessarily as simple as it seems. I know on my own journey towards living my Integrity, I still have moments, days even, where I feel disconnected from my truth, off-my-centre if you will. When I first released the free e-course for FIERCE Integrity, a person from India signed up and engaged into a dialogue via email with me. One particular day, I was feeling way out of my centre and I received an email from this person. The tag line at the end of their email said simply, "Everything is okay in the end. If it is not okay, it is not the end." These simple words were enough to pull me out of my story that day and realign me with my truth. What an enormous gift.

LESSON 20:

Integrity Champions

You know by now that at least part of this journey is about being open to receiving the gifts that surround you. It's about being willing and open to changing your perspective. One of the tools that has helped me to stay on my path towards living with Integrity has been to hold a space in my life for what I call my "Integrity Champions." These are the people who I have either met in real life or whose written words I have allowed to permeate my being, to essentially change my consciousness. I have opened myself to receiving their wisdom and knowledge and made a commitment to integrating it within my own life. I have done what I am asking you to do; take what resonates and leave out what doesn't.

In my own journey, I am first and foremost a lifelong student. Similar to the quote I just shared with you, about everything being okay in the end, I subscribe to the belief that "If I wake up in the morning, I'm not done!"—meaning that there are more lessons that I have yet to learn. When I get off track, or out of my heart-centre, one of the tools that I use to bring me back is my list of Integrity Champions. Some of the people on my list are people that I know well (my mom for example), and others are people who I only know through their writing (people like Louise Hay and Eckhart Tolle).

Questions for reflection:

- Who are your "Integrity Champions"?
- Who are the people who you admire and respect for their Integrity and Authenticity?

Action:

- Aside from the Integrity Champions that you know personally, if you are interested in reading some of the works that I have read, I have composed a list of authors/books at the back of the book for you to look at. As always, take what resonates, leave the rest!
- Come back to these inspiring people when you find yourself out of your centre!

NOTES LESSON 20

MAREN HASSE

LESSON 21:

Defining Success

As this course draws to a close, Lesson 21 is about reflecting on the journey and evaluating the outcome. Let's dive right in with some questions to get the reflection process started.

QUESTIONS FOR REFLECTION:

- Did you enjoy this project? Why or why not?
- What were the highs and lows of this course? Where would you say that you experienced the most success? What did you find the most challenging?
- Did you learn anything new about yourself? Did you have any epiphanies or a-ha moments?
- Has your ability to get into touch with the voice in your head improved at all?
- Are you finding that you are able to be kinder towards yourself and others?
- Have you noticed any changes in your patterns or habits?
- Has your speech changed?
- Have any of your relationships changed?
- What will you take away from this project?

- Re-connect with your intentions; have they been fulfilled?
- Would you say that you have been successful in your journey towards living with FIERCE Integrity?
- What is your plan going forward?

If, while you are reflecting on the course, you find that you have been able to make some changes stick but not others, not to worry! Remember that this is a process. One of the gifts of committing to this process as a lifelong journey is that it will continue to work! If you continue to work towards living with FIERCE Integrity, you can be sure that the Universe will continue to show you your "stuff", all of the things in you that you still need to heal. I call these "our onions." And what do onions have? Layers! I would say that the "goal" of this whole process is not to wake up tomorrow and live with 100% Integrity, but continue to do your best as you work towards it.

Along the way, know that you are going to fall down. You are going to screw up sometimes. You are. Accept that! The key is to make yourself vulnerable in these moments. Be willing to mess up so that you can learn from it, and don't forget to immediately forgive yourself when you do!

Our greatest lessons can come from our biggest failures. Being vulnerable is often uncomfortable; however, from my experience, the discomfort lasts for only a short time and the results are often totally worth it! Perhaps one of the greatest examples of being truly vulnerable in the human experience is to fall in love. When we allow ourselves to fall madly, hopelessly in love with someone, we are opening ourselves up to receiving love in return—but we are also at risk being hurt and heartbroken. Most people would agree that it is worth the risk!

I believe that the work that we are doing can have a life-changing effect, but it is important to remember that you aren't going to change your thoughts and behaviours overnight. This is going to take some time. In fact, I have used the expression, "This is my life's work." That is what I view the FIERCE Integrity Project to be for me—my life's work. A life-long project that will continue as long as I am alive. Because I can always improve, I can always be more authentic, I can always be more thoughtful. I can always live with an even greater sense of Integrity. In fact, one of my lifelong intentions is to wake up each day and be "more of me" than I was the day before.

How do I do this without getting totally overwhelmed? I do my best. That is all that I am asking you to do here, show up and do your best. A phrase that I use whenever I notice that I am being hard on myself or telling myself that I am not enough is "All I can do, is all I can do." I can't do/be more than I AM in that moment. All I can do is be me...and that is enough. If you can stand in your heart-centre and know this fundamental truth, that you are enough, then you are living with FIERCE Integrity.

"I never had a policy; I have just tried to do my very best each and every day."
~ *Abraham Lincoln*

Notes Lesson 21

CONCLUSION

Throughout this book, I have been sharing with you my own journey into living with FIERCE Integrity. As you have seen, I had been living out of my Integrity for much of my life and although I knew that something needed to change, I had no idea what it was or how to change it. As a result, I experienced a great deal of suffering, which I can now see was almost entirely self-inflicted. By buying into the voice in my head and the victim-mentality that existed there, I didn't believe that I had any control over my happiness.

We have seen that control of external events is a complete illusion. We can no more control what happens all around us than we could control the gravitational pull of the Earth. What we do have control over is how we think, how we react, and how we feel. By changing the voice in our heads, we can see the world through different eyes. This simple realization has the ability to end a great deal of your perceived suffering!

The best way that I know of to "stay the course" on this journey is to set your intentions. I have a written a lengthy document that delineates each and every expectation that I have for myself, my loved ones, and my life. Each and every day, as often as possible, I connect with the spirit of those intentions, and therefore I am continually working towards manifesting them into existence.

Another strategy that has helped me to stay on track is to surround myself with people who unconditionally love and support me. (Remember your "fantastic five"? You might want to re-think those people if you can't say the same about them.) These are the people in my life who keep bringing me back to my intentions and help me in striving to do my best.

This course is about cultivating awareness in your life. It is about being willing and open to receive so that you can return to your heart-centre as soon as possible. It is about forgiveness…forgiving yourself for buying into the story that took you out of your truth in the first place. If your intention is to live from your place of truth, from a place of FIERCE Integrity, then you can't fail. You might fall down, but you won't fail. In the end, you will spend more and more time in your heart and less and less time in your head. You will slowly transcend all of the stories in your head. And one day, when you least expect it, you will look down and you will be different…and that is a beautiful thing! Shanti, Om.

> *"Nothing is at last sacred but the integrity of your own mind."*
> ~ Ralph Waldo Emerson

ADDITIONAL NOTES

FIERCE *Integrity*

A COURSE IN LIVING YOUR TRUTH

RESOURCES AND REFERENCES

(aka some of my "Integrity Champions")

WEBSITES:

The Receiving Project: http://www.receivingproject.com

FIERCE Integrity e-Course, available at: www.marenhasse.com

The Work of Byron Katie: http://www.thework.com

BOOKS:

A course in miracles. S.l.: Foundation for Inner Peace, 1975.

Cameron, Julia. The artist's way: a spiritual path to higher creativity. Los Angeles, CA: Jeremy P. Tarcher/Perigee, 1992.

Dyer, Wayne W. Wishes fulfilled: mastering the art of manifesting. Carlsbad, Calif.: Hay House, 2012.

Hay, Louise L. You can heal your life. Santa Monica, CA: Hay House, 1987.

Hulnick, H. Ronald, and Mary R. Hulnick. Loyalty to your soul: the heart of spiritual psychology. Carlsbad, Calif.: Hay House, 2010.

Ruiz, Miguel. The four agreements: a practical guide to personal freedom. San Rafael, Calif.: Amber-Allen Pub.: 1997.

Tipping, Colin C. Radical forgiveness: making room for the miracle. 2nd ed. Marietta, GA: Global 13 Publishers, 2002.

Tolle, Eckhart. The power of now: a guide to spiritual enlightenment. Novato, Calif.: New World Library, 1999.

MAREN HASSE

ABOUT THE AUTHOR

Maren Hasse is dedicated to living a life with FIERCE Integrity. She serves as a life coach, author and workshop facilitator. Maren guides her clients to stunning personal transformation, as she assists them in taking down any barriers that stand in the way of reaching their full potential. She is available for one-to-one coaching, group classes, retreats, speaking engagements, and seminars. Maren is also the creator and facilitator of the free e-course FIERCE Integrity, and maintains a blog, which are both available through her website www.marenhasse.com.

Curious by nature, Maren loves to experience new things, including traveling, outdoor pursuits, and meeting different people. She feels content and fortunate to live with her husband Trent and their son Chephren in Stony Plain, Alberta, Canada, but is ever-open to the possibility of yet another adventure, especially if it involves time in the sun.

Photo Credit: Evan Noble

Made in the USA
Charleston, SC
16 June 2013